on PATTERN

Spectacular Quilts from Traditional Blocks

The Quilt Digest Press

Copyright © 1991 by Ruth B. McDowell.
All rights reserved. Published in the United States of America
by The Quilt Digest Press.

Editorial and production direction by Harold Nadel.
Book and cover design by Kajun Graphics, San Francisco.
Photography by Sharon Risedorph, San Francisco.
Typographical composition by DC Typography, San Francisco.
Printed by Nissha Printing Company, Ltd., Kyoto, Japan.
Color separations by the printer.

All quilts designed and made by the author; all diagrams by the author.

First printing.

Library of Congress Cataloging-in-Publication Data

McDowell, Ruth B., 1945–
    Pattern on pattern : spectacular quilts from traditional blocks /
Ruth B. McDowell.
    p. cm.
   ISBN 0-913327-31-X (ppr) : $19.95
    1. Quilting—Patterns.   2. Patchwork—Patterns.   I. Title.
TT835.M276   1991
746.9'7—dc20   90-29178
                                      CIP

The Quilt Digest Press
P.O. Box 1331
Gualala, California 95445

I n dedicating this book, I would like to acknowledge especially the contributions of Nancy Halpern and Rhoda Cohen. Their work inspired me to begin making my own designs in the first place, and their continuing generosity and support have been invaluable to me ever since.

Sylvia Einstein and Barbara Crane have been a constant joy. Thanks also to Karen Lauterwasser and to the many other people who have encouraged me to pursue this work.

Special thanks to the Rybicki family for their emotional support and technical expertise.

I would like to thank as well the Pfaff Co. for the use of a Pfaff 1473 CD sewing machine.

But, most of all, this book is dedicated to my daughters Emily and Leah, who have grown up in the midst of threads, common pins, snippets of cloth and piles of fabric, and who haven't complained even when there are tiny triangles of cloth

floating

in the bathtub.

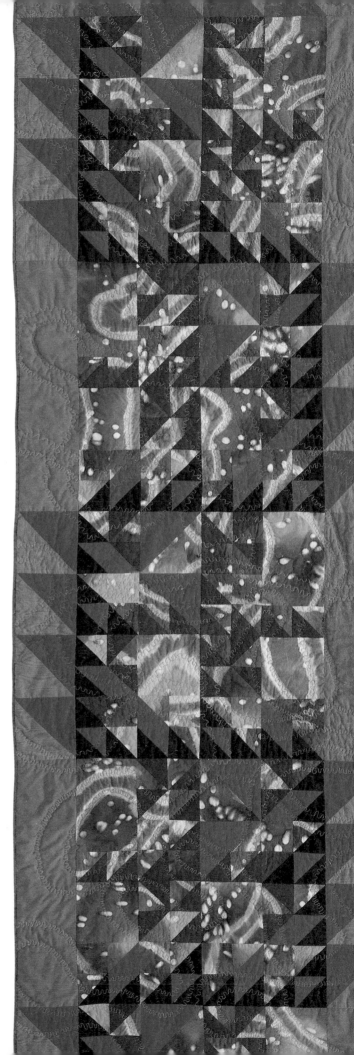

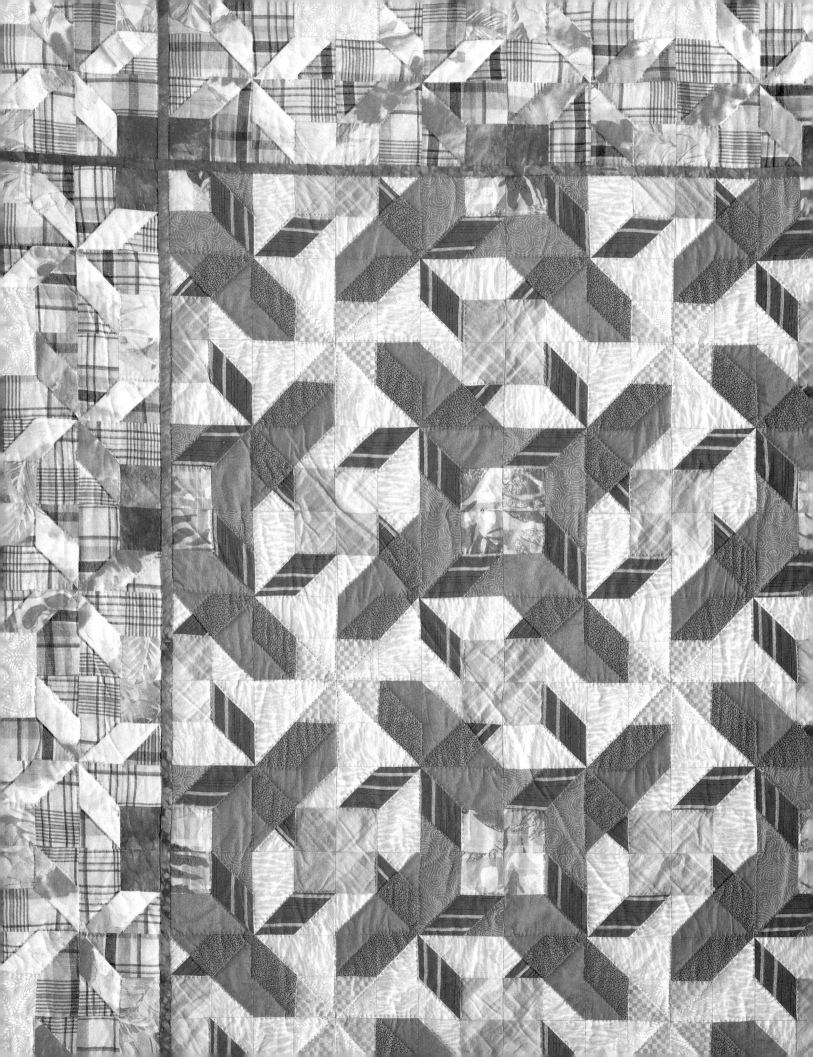

CONTENTS

Toss a stone into a pond. From the initial splash, concentric rings spread out further and further until they fade away. Look at a puddle in a shower of rain. Rings upon rings form and spread, overlapping each other, forever changing. Small circles, larger circles, the pattern echoes again and again, overlapping, intersecting, at different sizes, from different centers, making a complicated and beautiful design.

In a similar way, we can create our own original surface patterns. The repetition of lines and other design elements creates visual echoes within the pattern. By varying the relative scales of the original pattern, the overlaps, their alignment and orientation, we can produce an infinity of pattern. The pattern reverberates in a simple way, or with great complexity.

I first became aware of the possibilities of this kind of reverberant design while investigating types of tiling patterns. Then, as a quiltmaker, I focused on the traditional quilt block patterns.

This book presents twenty new quilts based on simple traditional blocks, given greater design complexity by the use of reverberant pattern. In addition, there are two simple original block designs which I hope will encourage you to try your own.

The process of developing reverberant pattern includes many variables: different scales of the same pattern; relative sizes; amount of overlap; whether any lines coincide. Color and texture are also variables. Will the various scales of pattern be treated as transparencies or not? Quilting stitches can be treated as the introduction of a line drawing on the surface. Should the pattern of quilting stitches be yet another scale of the original pattern? At what size, what orientation, by hand or machine, with what thread color(s)?

In designing the quilts for this book, I chose to use relatively simple traditional pieced blocks. The quilts are intended as examples of simple approaches to working with reverberant patterning. Templates and yardages are given for all but two of them. The examples in the book are intended to stimulate your interest in reverberant patterns, encouraging you to create exciting original designs.

Although I have often used solid colors, in some instances I have chosen some very unusual commercially available prints to encourage you to look for off-beat fabrics and to begin to experiment with them in your work. The fabrics that work best for me in most cases are not "pretty" prints. A variety of scale of prints, different printed or woven combinations of colors, and a wide selection of types of figured patterns can combine to give your quilts richness and complexity of visual texture.

Finally, in completing these quilts and writing this book, I feel that I have only rippled the surface of reverberant patterning. The possibilities seem endless for quiltmakers of all levels. I hope that the simple idea of reverberant pattern will be the stone in the water that will set off echoes in original and fascinating quilts yet to be made.

Part 1
GENERAL INFORMATION

DESIGN CONSIDERATIONS

Reverberant Patterns

Reverberant pattern designing can be handled in several ways. First select a quilt block from which to work. Repeat the block to form an overall pattern. Draw the same pattern at a larger scale, **on tracing paper**. A simple doubling of the size of the original drawing is a good place to start.

You will be able to slide the second drawing back and forth, or flip it over, or tip it at an angle to experiment with design possibilities. With access to a good copy machine, you can have transparencies (acetates) made of your original line drawing at different enlargements and reductions. Experiment with overlapping two or more of these transparencies in different ways to see what patterns develop. Line drawings can also be developed, enlarged or reduced, tilted or overlapped on some home computers.

Some of the variations illustrated in this book are:

I have chosen reverberant pattern designs for this book with an eye on simple construction and a limited number of templates. Some patterns are made from only three templates. Others use more. A few are fascinating, but technically extraordinarily difficult to construct by piecing. They are included as an inspiration and challenge.

If two different scales of pattern are chosen, they can be overlapped in a number of ways. The first drawing on page 81 illustrates the overlap selected for my *Clay's Choice* quilt. Five alternate overlaps are also illustrated. There is a sixth option that would require significantly more templates on page 82. Tracing paper, transparencies and/or a computer are convenient for exploring these possibilities.

Transparency

Overlapping line drawings is one method of dealing with reverberant pattern. Overlapping colored designs and treating the colors as though they were transparent is another. That you can, by careful choice of color, value and pattern, make adjacent pieces of fabric appear to overlap each other is an exciting process. At the most basic level, you can experiment with colors by overlapping pieces of transparent colored plastic or glass. Yellow and blue make green. Red and blue make purple. In fabric, *Mill Wheel I* (page 40) demonstrates this most directly.

As you begin to experiment with transparency effects in fabrics, you will find it easiest to start with solid colors, which are easy to find in fabric stores. In addition to considering hue (color: red, yellow, blue, etc.), you must be careful with value (lightness or darkness) and intensity (how bright or saturated the color is). For instance, in *Merry-go-round* (page 76), small red-purple triangles overlap large blue triangles. For the transparent overlap, I used a purple fabric. The purple is about right in hue and intensity, but a little too dark in value to make the transparency work well. We cannot always achieve perfection.

Transparency can also be made to work with patterned fabrics. *Maple Leaf* (page 35) has printed reds, blues and purples mixed with the solids. The strong colors, however, are much more significant visual elements than the little bit of patterning in the fabrics, so the use of printed fabrics here is really incidental to the vivid color transparency.

With *Birds in the Air* (page 53), however, the transparency works perfectly both in the black/white/blue transparency and in the printed designs of pine branches and bamboo. It looks as though a clear blue film were placed over parts of a quilt that had been pieced entirely from two black and white fabrics. In fact, the perceived transparency was created by using two colorways of the same printed fabric: black-and-white and navy-and-blue pine branches and bamboo.

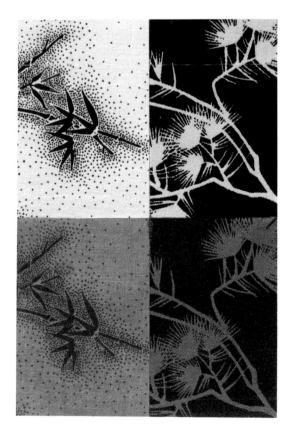

Birds in the Air

Roman Square (next page)

For *Roman Square* (page 102), I was able to find two printed fabrics of almost the same scale and design, but one was black and off-white and the other gray and lavender. Combined with two almost solid fabrics in the smaller-scale blocks, these two produce a satisfying transparency effect.

Roman Square assumes more complexity in the border, where there is a deviation from the established transparency relationship. At the top border, the smaller-scale pattern is treated as though it were opaque and on top of the larger diagonal bars. At the bottom of the border, the diagonal pattern is opaque and on top of the smaller one. This same idea was exploited in *Prairie Queen* (page 120), but in the body of the quilt rather than in the border.

Transparency has been utilized to varying degrees throughout these quilts. Some are near-perfect transparencies, some only partial. In some quilts, for example *Roman Square Pinwheels* (page 108), transparency is not used at all.

FABRICS

Fabric Selection

The process of fabric selection is the most absorbing aspect of quiltmaking for me. It requires intense concentration and just a lot of looking. For a large or complicated quilt, it can mean having to make hundreds of difficult interlocking decisions. Using many different types of fabrics well is a much more difficult process than limiting your choices to a single type, but if you can keep your eyes open and your inhibitions in check, it can lead you into new, exciting and unexpected directions.

Solids vs. Prints

It is interesting to compare the quilts composed mainly of solid colors with those constructed of plaids and prints. The use of large-scale printed and plaid fabrics in quilts such as *Clay's Choice*, *Jacob's Ladder II* and *Roman Square Pinwheels* makes designs in which the pieced elements blend together, forming a complex, unified surface.

The solid colors in *Mill Wheel I* and *Four Patch* variation define and emphasize the graphic nature of the pieced design. In these two quilts, each piece of fabric remains discrete.

Calicoes

Tiny calico prints act somewhat like lively solids when used in quilts. The small scale of the printed design tends to keep the outline of each piece distinct. The tiny prints do, however, add a visual texture that is missing from solid-color fabrics. It is especially important to consider each piece of calico carefully from a distance as well as close up. It is easy to be seduced by a small swatch of calico, only to find that from a distance the fabric is overly busy and distracting.

Visual Texture, Tactile Texture and Reflectivity

Many fabrics with the same tactile texture may have very different visual textures, depending on the type of surface pattern used on them, its scale, colors, amount of contrast, type of lines, figuration, etc. They *look* as if they would feel different.

Fabrics with very different tactile textures, for instance muslin, satin, denim, velveteen and raw silk, may have very different visual textures as well. They may also reflect light in different ways—be shiny like lamé or highly glazed cotton, or satiny, or completely matte like flannel.

Choices in visual texture, tactile texture and reflectivity are made in selecting fabrics, in addition to consideration of hue (color), value (lightness or darkness), and intensity (brightness or saturation). The choice to work exclusively with solid-color cotton fabrics allows you to concentrate on color by deliberately eliminating most consideration of visual texture, tactile texture and reflectivity. It is one of many available options for fabric selection and, for a first quilt made from this book, it may be the place to start.

Iridescent Fabrics and Chambrays

Another type of fabric to consider is woven with one color in the weft and a different color in the warp. Many Thai silks are made this way, and some cottons and drapery fabrics as well. In working with this fabric, by rotating pieces at different angles in a quilt you can produce wonderful, subtle color differences from piece to piece.

Napped fabrics can be treated in a similar way. Varying the angle at which you place the nap will cause differences in the perceived color of the pieces.

The hills and valleys created by the quilting stitches produce interesting color shifts as well on these kinds of fabrics. I have one nice cotton of a good quilting weight which appears to be brown, but which in fact is woven of a bright orange warp and a bright green weft.

Wrong Sides

Look at the wrong sides of your printed fabrics. Quite often the dyes come through the cloth at different rates and the wrong side may have a very different combination of colors than the front. Wrong sides are especially useful if you are trying to achieve a foggy or wintery look in a quilt, since they frequently have a frosty appearance.

In *Corn and Beans* (page 87), the wrong side of the sunflower fabric makes a significant contribution to defining the piecing pattern. Using the wrong side of an off-white/black calico print for the background fabric in *Roman Square* (page 102) gave me a background with a little visual texture that relates to the shaded bluish drapery fabric and the other black/off-white prints without adding too much figure to an area that should read as a solid.

Furnishing Fabrics

Many of the printed fabrics that I like to use come from drapery or furnishing bolts and remnants. They have some advantages over quilt fabrics in the variety of scales of pattern available as well as in the variety and combinations of colors and visual textures. Many of the printed designs are in subtle colorings, and many are available that do not use blossoms as their main design theme. Many furnishing fabrics are printed from eight or more colors, rather than the two or three in many quilt fabrics. They are also intentionally made to resist fading in strong light.

The main drawback to the use of furnishing fabric in quilts is their heavier weight. I have sucessfully used many different weights of fabrics together in the same quilt, and I don't find that working with them presents unusual technical difficulties. It must, of course, be said that heavier fabrics are much more difficult to quilt by hand.

Fabric Preparation

All of the fabrics I use in my work have been put through the rinse cycle of my washer, then in the drier, before being used for patchwork. In addition to weeding out those fabrics that run, this process removes the sizing and the chemical smell which is frequently present in new fabric. It will also tell you whether the glazed finish on a piece of cloth will disappear when the quilt is washed, a bit of information I would prefer to know before I consider how to use that cloth. Additionally, it will shrink those fabrics which are not already preshrunk.

The rinsing and drying process makes the fabrics softer, so they are more easily hand quilted. Twill fabrics are surprisingly easy to hand quilt. While they are heavy in ounces per yard, the threads are not packed closely together. The most difficult fabrics to deal with in hand quilting are those woven densely, like a 200-count sheet, with such tight threads that it is hard to get the needle through. While furnishing fabrics, owing to their weight, present some problems in hand quilting, I have found I am willing to tolerate this in order to get the patterns, colors and fade-resistance.

Washing fabrics before use may also remove soil-repellant finishes. There are pros and cons to every choice.

Quilting as a Salvage Art

I like the challenge of using "found" fabrics. Quilting has always been a salvage art. Indeed, much of the charm of antique quilts comes from working imaginatively with the fabrics that were at hand. I try to remember this when I run out of a fabric right in the middle of constructing a quilt. Although I am temporarily frustrated, combining things in a different way usually produces a more interesting quilt.

I like the richness and complexity of quilt surfaces made from many different patterned fabrics, which are reminders of the connections these fabrics have to other familiar parts of our lives.

Fabric Collection

Having a fabric collection to work from is vital to working out a careful color scheme. Your library of fabric is your palette. There are eras when no yellow/greens are manufactured, others no sky blues. Without a fabric collection to draw on, you will be limited in your choices to what the current market makes available. My fabric comes from many different sources, mostly a wide variety of small pieces.

Many of the fabrics that work most successfully for me are not "pretty" fabrics. I was fortunate as a beginning quiltmaker to be able to study at close hand the fabric choices Rhoda Cohen and Nancy Halpern were making for their work. Some of the world's "ugliest" fabrics are found in their wonderful quilts.

Expanding one's fabric choices requires taking considerable risks, but not usually heavy expenditures. Acquiring a small piece of an "impossible" fabric and learning to use it well is a big growth step.

To Dye or Not to Dye

Hand-dyeing fabric is certainly one way of assuring control of your available colors; unfortunately, there may be a tendency to overvalue them simply because they were dyed by your hand. I prefer not to use paint or dye myself, but to make my quilts from the wide selection of "found" fabrics.

Sometimes, when I am working on an especially complicated piece, I can't tell before the quilt is assembled whether all of the fabric choices are exactly right. For small adjustments to an almost completed piece, I either remove a piece of fabric with a seam ripper and replace it with another, better choice—by machine if I'm dealing with just the quilt top, or by hand if the quilting has already been done. Or I appliqué small pieces of fabric to the surface to adjust the final design. (When appliquéing, it is best to cut away as much of the fabric covered by the appliqué as possible. This will help to make the appliqué recede into the surface of the quilt rather than riding on top of it like a patch.) Or, as in the center of *Double T* (page 155), where I wanted that particular piece of fabric in that particular spot but found that it needed modification, I made necessary color/value adjustments with fabric paint.

Most fabric choices are, finally, personal preferences. Who you are and what you like are individual statements that you can make in your quilt. As you grow and change, your fabric choices will change, too. They celebrate the diversity of their makers now, as they have always done.

PREPLANNING

How Much Preplanning is Enough?

Some quiltmakers prefer to draft the whole quilt on paper, including borders, and color it in with paint or pencil before beginning to sew. I find that the change in scale from a paper drawing to a full-size quilt, and the change in color quality from pencil or paint to fabric, can throw off the balance of the whole design.

I have also designed some lovely quilts on paper, only to find that the colors I had chosen were unavailable in fabric. It is especially difficult to make a definitive drawing when printed and patterned fabrics will be used in the quilt.

All of my quilts now begin with either a line drawing of the block or a full-size line drawing of the entire quilt. To the drawing, I then begin to add my fabrics. The fabric choices are made as I actually cut the pieces. The design wall (see page 28 for details) is invaluable at this stage, although it is possible to pin pieces to a white sheet as a temporary solution.

TECHNICAL CONSIDERATIONS

Templates

Twenty of the quilts in this book are accompanied by full-size templates. Each template is identified with a quilt name and template number. The templates are drawn with a dotted line which represents the seam line and a solid line which will be the cutting line, leaving ¼" seam allowance.

In some cases a template will be used wrong side up to cut a reversed or mirrored piece. This will be indicated by the letter R on the template maps and tables.

In a few instances, where templates are too large to be included in this book, they are diagrammed at small scale with full-size measurements given. The measurements will determine the *seam* line. The notation ASATAS means to Add (¼") Seam Allowances To All Sides of each piece. Draw a line ¼" *outside* all measured seam lines, and use this for the cutting line.

When piecing right triangles together with squares, it is easier to line the pieces up correctly if the points of the triangles are cut off. Both cutting lines are drawn on the templates to allow choice.

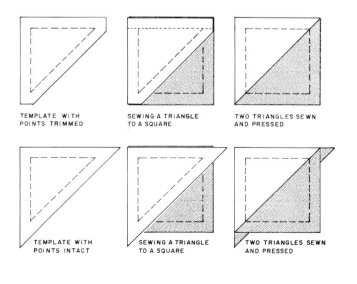

TEMPLATE WITH POINTS TRIMMED

SEWING A TRIANGLE TO A SQUARE

TWO TRIANGLES SEWN AND PRESSED

TEMPLATE WITH POINTS INTACT

SEWING A TRIANGLE TO A SQUARE

TWO TRIANGLES SEWN AND PRESSED

When I am going to use a template over and over again, I cut it out of plastic. It makes a long-lasting, transparent template.

For very accurate piecing, especially with long, skinny points, I mark a dot on the template at critical points and punch a hole in the template with a paper punch. The paper punch I use is a standard scissors-type punch that punches a 1/8″ hole. (Most normal punches make a 1/4″ hole.) I found mine at a regular stationery store. A small hole can also be made in plastic templates with a heated needle. Marking a dot on the fabric through the hole allows me to pin together two pieces right at the dot, so that they match exactly when pieced.

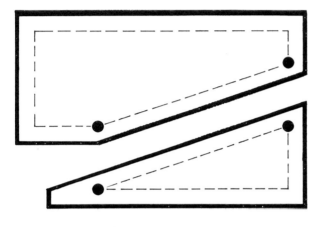

Graph-paper Templates

For very complex designs, where many templates are required, but each one will be used only a few times, I use 16 lb. technical tracing vellum from an architect's supply store. An example of a quilt made in this way is *Double T* (page 155). A 20 lb. vellum is also available, more expensive but stiffer.

The vellum I use has an 8-to-the-inch grid printed on it in light blue ink. Other grid sizes are available. It comes in sheets, pads and rolls in various sizes up to 42″ wide by 20 yards long. While it is not inexpensive, it is less expensive than template plastic, the grid is very accurate, and you can trace through it.

The 16 lb. vellum is stiff enough that, with care, you can trace around pieces a few times. I usually do this on the ironing board, stabbing a few

straight pins through the vellum and the fabric into the ironing board to hold the template in place while I trace around it. Since the ironing board is higher than an ordinary table, this method has the added advantage that it is easier on your back.

Piecing

I do all my piecing on the sewing machine. It is a method that I have used from the beginning and that I feel very comfortable with. Other quilters piece by hand. These are two very different **processes**. Which you prefer will be an individual choice, depending on your personal preferences, the physical circumstances, the type of quilt you are constructing and the fabrics being used. I don't find one method inherently "better" than the other. With skill, machine piecing can be every bit as accurate and precise as hand piecing.

Within the pieced blocks in some of these quilts, you may find smaller units such as four-patches or squares made from two triangles. The construction of the overall blocks can be simplified by sewing these "sub-assembly" units first. There are a number of machine quick-piecing techniques which can speed up these simple constructions. Two are illustrated here. With both of these methods, mark the triangles and squares on the top strip of fabric, using the templates given in this book.

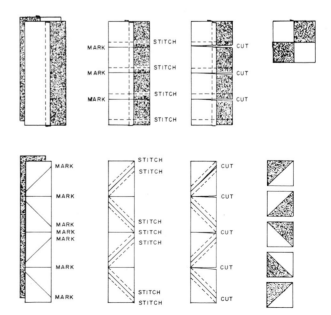

For piecing curved seams such as in the *Mill Wheel* quilts (pages 40 and 45), you will need to clip the seam allowance on the concave piece. Mark the curves at the dots indicated on the templates and pin the corresponding dots together along the seam lines as well as at the ends of the seams. When piecing curves on the machine, put the concave piece on top and spread out the clips so that the fabric edges match.

Sewing Machines

Any sewing machine with a good straight stitch and back stitch can be used for piecing quilts. A back stitch will be very useful in piecing "Y" seams.

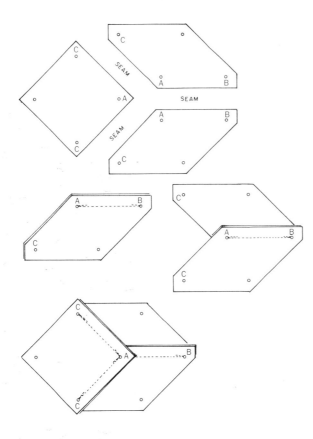

Newer machines have convenience features you may find useful. I especially appreciate:

A built-in even-feed foot

Feed dogs that can be dropped

A switch to stop the needle in the fabric or out of the fabric

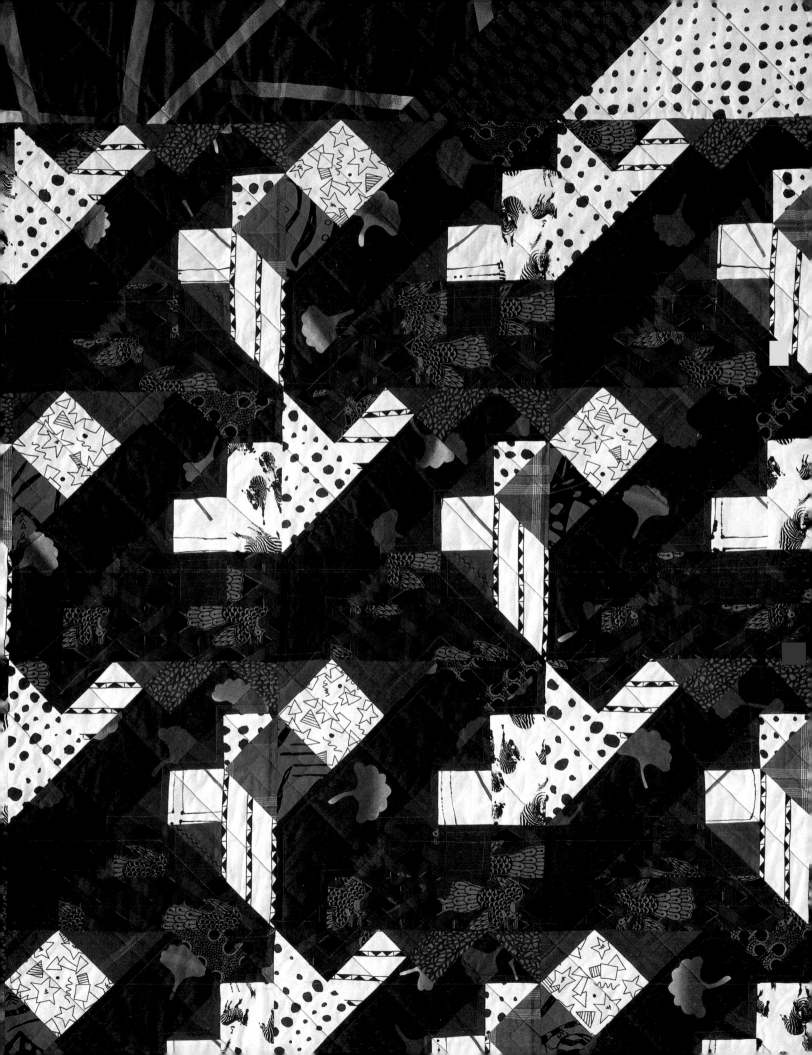

Slow and fast speed
Variable needle position, side to side
Easily adjustable tension
A switch to tie off the beginning or end of a seam
  or pattern
Programmable stitches for machine quilting.

Angled Seams

Most of the quilts illustrated in this book are based on traditional patterns. They are assembled with right angle or 45-degree angle seams. It is perfectly possible, though, to piece seams at any angle desired. With careful sewing, the quilts come out fine. It is a good idea, if possible, to keep the grain of the fabric aligned with the edge of the block. This will keep the blocks square and make them easier to sew together.

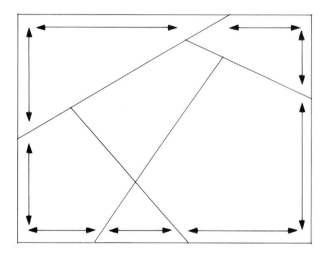

Pressing

There are many different ways to handle the pressing of the seams in a quilt. Some quiltmakers crease the seams only with finger pressure; others use a steam or dry iron. I personally use a steam iron most of the time and press both seam allowances to the same side. Pressing seams open may make them more difficult to repair if they rip, may allow batting to beard up along the seam, and does make it difficult to quilt in the ditch. But it does make elegant flat tops and cuts down on bulk in some complicated piecing situations. One of my friends presses her seam allowances open, and her tops lie as flat as flat can be. You decide.

Borders

Borders are difficult.

A border is not simply a frame for a quilt. A well-designed border can make a good quilt much better. A creative border can rescue a boring center. But designing the border presents a whole new series of decisions you may not find the energy to undertake. It's so easy to slap the same fabric to all four sides and call it done; but, if you are willing to make that last effort, your work will benefit.

You will find a number of different approaches to borders in this book.

Color change in outer row of blocks:

One scale of pattern used alone as a border:

Design element from the center used in a different way:

No border at all:

Incomplete overlap of patterns:

Different transparency effect:

Different size of pattern block:

Composed border:

Sometimes the border can help resolve the color problems encountered at the pieced center. *Maple Leaf* (page 35) could have been a completely different quilt with a more restrained border. *Fire on the Mountain* (page 60) is made even hotter by that ashy border. The mustard border on *Birds in the Air* (page 53) complements the blue/black/white center. Those cranberry red corner blocks are very important to *Corn and Beans* (page 87).

It is interesting to mask out the borders on the color plates with white paper to see the impact of the borders. Alternately, mask out the center and imagine a new center to go with the remaining border. I know two wonderful contemporary quilts that were designed from the outside in.

Planning a Special Border

I usually begin planning a border by pinning my pieced center to an eight foot by eight foot design wall (see page 28) in my studio and studying it for a while. Then I select a few fabrics that I think may work, fold them to what seems like the right size and pin them up next to the pieced center. After studying them for a while, I change some, try others, combine them in different ways until I arrive at a border composition that enhances the quilt.

I am frequently surprised in the process of choosing a border and will end up with something entirely different from my initial idea. The process becomes a kind of visual dialogue between me and the evolving quilt. It requires great concentration. Don't rush: spread the process out to help resolve your indecisions. If you have room, leave the quilt up where you can see it as you walk by for a few days (or weeks) to help you decide whether the final design works or not.

Measuring for Borders

When adding a border to a pieced center, measure across the center of the quilt in both directions. Use these measurements for the border rather than relying on careful mathematics. Pieced tops frequently turn out slightly larger or smaller than planned.

Butted vs. Mitered Corners

I prefer butted corners on borders in most circumstances. It is a straightforward approach which defines the separate elements in the con-

struction process. I sew mitered corners on borders only where they echo a mitering process in the body of the quilt.

Basting

In preparing a quilt sandwich, when getting ready for the quilting process, I have abandoned thread basting. Basted quilts, in my experience, shift during the quilting process. I prefer to pin-baste my tops, batting and backing together, using 1⅜" long glass-headed extra-fine straight pins and taking two "stitches" with each pin.

The two stitches hold the pins in place more securely. Safety pins have been recommended for this process because they won't slip out accidentally and they won't scratch. I find the process of fastening 350 safety pins so painful that I prefer the straight-pin method, being careful how I handle the quilt and putting up with a few scratches.

With the pinning method, you must of course use caution, when stretching the quilt in a hoop, not to jam the top hoop down over a pin and tear the cloth.

When pinning a quilt to be machine quilted, determine in advance in which direction the quilt will be rolled to fit under the arm of the machine. Inserting all of the straight pins to point along the length of the roll will create less of a porcupine.

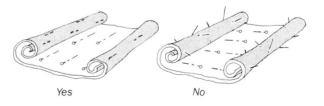

Yes   No

I have found that pin-basting works so well at holding the layers in place that I am able, with hand or machine quilting, to quilt just enough to hold the quilt together (lines about four inches apart), remove most of the pins, then go back and finish filling in the quilting.

The choice of which method to use in your work, basting with thread, safety pins or straight pins, is up to you and will depend on your methods of working and your personal preferences.

Quilting

The quilting design is really a pattern of lines which are added to a fabric surface. The lines will hold the layers together and, because of the batting, will add a relief dimension to the surface.

Studying line patterns is very helpful in designing quilting. Spend some time doodling. How many different kinds of cross-hatched patterns can you develop? Invent patterns of meanders, smooth swoops, broken lines, zig zags. All of these could be used in the quilting process.

Traditionally, quilting has been done by hand with a tiny running stitch and cotton thread. This produces a line which is very soft and indistinct. Quilting on a sewing machine produces a line that is much crisper and more definite. The type of quilting to use is determined by what visual effect I want the piece to have.

Hand Quilting

I like to hand quilt. I do all of my own hand quilting. I like the change of pace. Designing and piecing are intense and mentally exhausting. Hand quilting is meditative and gives me time to slow down, to think about the quilt I have been working on, what I learned from it, and what I will be doing next.

Hand quilting can be done in various ways: in a frame, in a hoop, without any aids; with a metal thimble, two metal thimbles, leather thimble, no thimble; using different types of needles; using cotton quilting thread, metallic thread, silk or rayon thread, variegated thread; using a running stitch, back stitch, small stitches, big stitches. Once you develop skill in hand quilting, all the options are available. All will give different visual effects to the quilted surface.

Machine Quilting

Machine quilting also offers a wealth of possibilities. There are even some methods of machine quilting using a transparent thread on top, cotton thread on the bobbin, and a tight top tension, to mimic hand quilting. I prefer to be more straightforward and let the machine quilting look like machine quilting.

Some possibilities are:

Thread:
Cotton (many sizes)
Variegated cotton (many sizes)
Transparent nylon (clear or smoke)
Silk or silk buttonhole twist
Rayon
Metallic
Yarn

Stitches:
Straight
Straight, twin or triple needle
Zig zag
Programmed stitches
Self-programmed stitches
Any combination of the above.

Tying

The other traditional method of fastening the layers together is some variety of tying. Many quilts have been tied with heavy cotton thread or yarn and square knots. There are sophisticated versions of this in which the ties themselves form a major design element. There are hand-tufting techniques which give a different visual effect from hand-running-stitch quilting but leave no ends showing. You can take two small backstitches to form each tuft, then slide the needle through the batting to the next stitch point.

In the *Snowflake* quilt (page 127), the outer edges were fastened with machine-stitched programmed snowflakes which give the effect of randomly spaced quilted polka dots. I have heard of the same technique being done with machine-stitched buttonholes treated both as a design element and as an interesting way to tie the quilt together.

Quilt-as-you-go

In machine quilting, the technically difficult part lies in fitting the bulk of the quilt under the arm of the machine. That can be simplified to some extent by assembling and quilting the piece in smaller sections.

Quilt-as-you-go Method 1: Assemble the top, batting and backing for each section of the quilt separately. Machine quilt each entire section. Trim the batting close to the seam line. Machine piece the quilted sections together through all layers. Cover the seams on the back by hemming straight or bias fabric strips over them by hand.

Quilt-as-you-go Method 2: Assemble the top, batting and backing for each section separately. Machine quilt the sections, stopping an inch or two from the edges that will be joined together. Trim the batting very slightly smaller than the top. Trim the back ¼″ larger than the top. Machine piece the top sections together, leaving the batting and backing free. Smooth together the edges of the batting. From the back, smooth one piece of the backing over the other, turn under the edge and hem the backs together by hand. Finish the quilting in the area over the joining seam. See the *Snowflake* quilt (page 127) for a more detailed discussion.

Method 1 works best for quilting designs that are planned to extend all the way to the edge of each section. Method 2 works best where most of the quilting can be done in the body of the piece and the edge quilting worked later.

Machine Quilting with the Regular Presser Foot

King's Crown (page 113) and *Maple Leaf* (page 35) were quilted on my old sewing machine along relatively simple straight-line patterns, using a regular presser foot and feed dogs. In addition to the basting pins, I pinned each line just before it was stitched with a row of straight pins 1½ to 2 inches apart. This extra pinning keeps the layers in place and prevents any pleats from forming on the fronts or backs. Machine quilting with a regular presser foot does work, although such quilting is much more easily done with an even-feed or walking foot.

Machine Quilting with an Even-feed Foot

Even-feed feet are built into some new sewing machines and are available as an accessory for many older machines. They replace the regular presser foot. With an even-feed foot, the presser foot walks along the top fabric in the same way that the feed dogs walk along the bottom fabric. It eliminates the need for extra pinning along a line of machine quilting, because the top and backing move at the same rate. An even-feed foot is also very useful in sewing a binding to a finished quilt.

Free-motion Quilting

I have recently begun exploring free-motion quilting which, on my twenty-five-year-old machine, is done with a darning foot and feed-dog cover plate. The darning foot moves up and down with the needle. It holds the fabric in place only when the needle is actually in the fabric. With the feed dogs covered, you can move the quilt, and therefore the line of stitching, in any direction and at any speed you want. A rather firm backing fabric helps this process.

Many newer machines have a switch that allows you to drop the feed dogs for free-motion stitching.

A large, clear, flat work space is a necessity in machine quilting. Having the sewing machine set into a cabinet or table so that the bed of the machine is level with the working surface makes machine quilting much easier.

With a contrasting thread in the machine, it seems as though your sewing machine needle had turned into a pen. You can doodle in any direction.

Fire on the Mountain (page 60) is free-motion quilted in patterns of flames worked in horizontal bands. It would have been much easier to have used quilt-as-you-go, but I didn't. The quilting is a free-hand pattern of flames, without advance marking of the quilting lines.

Quilting by free motion on the home sewing machine in a pattern of this scale (the flames are about 18″ high on the bottom row) calls for a lot of repositioning of your hands. The meandering pattern in the border quilting is of a scale that is easier to handle mechanically. In free-motion quilting without previously marked lines, you have to anticipate visually what direction you are going next. It requires intense co-ordination to develop an even rhythm and to keep the piece moving in the right direction.

On the home sewing machine, you move the quilt to create the design. On a commercial quilting machine, the head of the machine is moved over the quilt.

Designing New Quilting Patterns

I have used the quilts in this book as an opportunity to explore many ways of handling the quilting designs for pieced quilts.

Beyond the traditional method, by hand in the ditch, there are:

All-over free-motion continuous line machine quilting:

Machine free-motion stipple quilting:

Machine free-motion drawing to complete design elements:

Machine free-motion quilting from the back:

Doodling with machine free-motion:

Machine straight-line quilting, regular presser foot:

Machine straight-line quilting, even-feed foot:

Machine quilting using another scale of the piecing design:

Using pre-programmed fancy stitches for machine quilting:

Using self-programmed machine fancy stitches:

Hand quilting:

Tying:

I am very interested in the idea of using the quilting lines to apply an unrelated free-hand drawing to a pieced geometric surface. The first time I saw this technique was in Nancy Halpern's *Falls Island, Reversing Falls* in 1979. Nancy had wanted to quilt a sinuous pattern of swirling lines across a geometric landscape. She found the geometry interfering with the freedom of the lines. So she turned the quilt over and hand quilted it from the back, a plainer surface. Only a hand quilter with stitches as beautiful as Nancy's could pull this off so well.

Nancy says she got the idea from an old pieced quilt formerly in the collection of Lenice Bacon. The front of the quilt was made of very large pieced blocks. The back of the quilt was plain unbleached muslin upon which the quiltmaker traced many different leaves from her yard, then quilted them with dark brown thread.

Machine quilting from the back is not technically difficult. I have experimented with this in quilts of my own, using plain backing fabric and drawing the quilting lines on the back. In *Shoo Fly* (page 141), I used a large-scale drapery print of foliage as the backing fabric. After machine free-motion quilting this piece from the back by outlining the printed design, I went back and filled in some areas with machine stipple quilting.

Quilting an Angled Grid

Here is a sketch for a quilt like *Double T* (page 155) with the quilting design drawn at a different scale and a different angle from the piecing design. Marking of this type of grid accurately is somewhat difficult, but it gives the work an added sophistication. One system that I have used involves pinning (or taping) the completed top to a large grid at an angle. In my case this was a 6" grid drawn on my design wall, but a tile floor or wall would work as well. By placing a long straight-edge across the quilt top from grid line to grid line, I was able to mark the pieced top accurately.

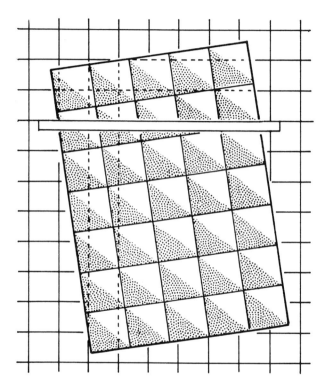

Experimenting with Quilting Patterns on Tracing Paper

It is difficult to imagine what a particular quilting design will look like on a particular top. Tracing paper can be very helpful. Good tracing paper is also available at an architect's supply store. It comes in rolls 12" to 42" wide by 50 yards long and is almost transparent. It is also very inexpensive.

Pin or tape your completed top to a wall and cover it completely with tracing paper. Experiment with pencil on the tracing paper, trying different quilting possibilities. You will be able to see the quilt top through the tracing paper well enough to help you make a decision before you start marking your top.

Marking Quilting Lines

I am not entirely happy with any of the methods I have tried to mark quilting lines. I don't trust "wash out" markers. I generally use a pencil (white or silver if necessary).

A system that works well, but can be used only just before a line is stitched, involves marking the line with a crease. Put the quilt down on a firm surface and trace over the line to be stitched with a hard, smooth edge, such as the back of a seam ripper or a Japanese *hera*. This makes a crisp crease to follow with your needle and does not leave any marking on the quilt surface.

The wheeled dispensers that use powdered chalk also work well to mark freehand quilting lines just before they are quilted.

I am trying to learn simply to draw quilting lines with the needle as I sew. This is a difficult process, but similar to learning to become adept at sketching with a pencil. I like the irregularity of lines drawn without the aid of a straight-edge or compass. It is interesting to invent a repertoire of filling patterns for both hand and machine quilting which can be stitched free-hand.

Design Wall

A design wall is a wonderful thing if you can arrange space for one. Mine is two 4 foot by 8 foot sheets of a soft gray wallboard from a building supply store fastened to the wall and painted white. I pin fabric pieces to my wall with straight pins. Some people cover a wall with flannel or fleece and depend on friction to hold the pieces in place. Plan to locate a design wall where you can stand back to assess the quilt at some distance. This is especially helpful if your work is large and its subdivisions cannot be taken in from up close.

Paper-faced foam illustration board from an art supply store makes a good portable board, as do some types of insulation panels. Some quilters fasten two panels together with a fabric hinge so they can be shut like a book and stored away.

Bindings

For wallhangings, I usually use a binding whose finished measurement is about ¼″ wide, cut from a straight-grain strip of cloth. In joining two pieces of binding together, lap them at right angles and stitch across the diagonal. Trim the excess and press the seam open. This will help avoid a lump where the strips are joined. An even-feed foot is helpful in sewing the raw edge of the binding to the quilt.

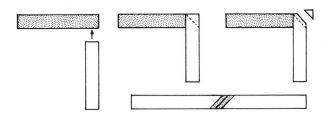

If any layer of your quilt is very easily stretched—for instance, contains bias edges—you may want to measure the length of the binding for each side of the quilt in the same manner recommended for borders (page 23).

Smoothing Out the Waves

It is the night before the quilt show, 2:00 AM, and you have just finished applying the binding. You hang your quilt up to admire its finished state, only to find the side edges waving back at you.

With a good strong quilting thread, tie a sturdy knot and put a row of hand quilting in the ditch along both sides of the quilt, just inside the binding. For a big quilt you may have to use several lengths of thread. Don't fasten off the ends of the threads yet. Hang the quilt as it will be hung in the show. Gently pull the quilting threads along each side to ease out the extra border fullness that is causing the waving. Fasten off all the threads well. In most cases, this little gathering won't show at all. For this invaluable technique, you should thank Barbara Lydecker Crane and her midnight inspiration.

Actually, this slight waving in the edges of wallhangings can happen to the most carefully pieced quilts. Sometimes it is due to the borders being slightly too long. Sometimes the quilting has been pulled too tight in some places. Be especially careful if some sections of your quilt have lots of quilting and some relatively little. The waving can be due to variability in the stretchiness of the fabrics used. The crosswise grain of many fabrics is very elastic, while the lengthwise grain has almost no stretch at all. You may want to take this into account in deciding whether to cut large pieces for a quilt from the crosswise or lengthwise grain. These problems are not usually noticeable when a quilt is used on a bed.

Folding Quilts

It is best to store a quilt flat (unfolded) in a dry, dark, well-ventilated space: not in a plastic bag, but covered with a washed cotton sheet.

If you have to fold a wallhanging for shipping or storage, make the first folds in a horizontal direction. When the quilt is hung, the weight of the quilt will tend to smooth out these horizontal folds. Try to unfold your quilts at regular intervals and refold them along other lines in order to prevent excessive wear from always creasing the cloth in the same place.

Enough of the technical information. Let's look at the quilts.

Part 2

THE QUILTS

HOW TO USE THIS SECTION

Each of the quilts in this book is described in a chapter of text. The quilts are sequenced by concept, rather than being arranged from the easiest to the most difficult: for example, *Maple Leaf* begins the series with a simple overlap; *Mill Wheel, Fire on the Mountain* and *Four Patch* variation use a variety of incomplete overlaps; *Merry-go-round* and *Clay's Choice* introduce the use of mirrored blocks.

Templates are given for the first twenty quilts. Each of these chapters also includes drawings that I call "template maps" and "color maps." A **template map** is a line drawing of the quilt (or quilt block) with **numbers** indicating which template to use for each piece. In a **color map**, the color of each piece is indicated with a **letter**. In some of the simpler quilts the color maps and template maps are combined on the same drawing.

If you wish to work with color transparencies, color AB should represent the overlap of color A and color B, color BC the overlap of color B and color C. If color transparency is not desired, choose any color you wish for AB or BC.

The descriptions of these first twenty quilts also contain **cutting tables** describing how many pieces of each fabric and each template you will need to cut to make the quilt as illustrated. A yardage figure is given for each fabric. This yardage figure represents the total yardage you will need to cut all of the pieces (and borders) of each fabric. For the large quilts, the borders are intended to be pieced to get the required length. Should you want to cut these long borders all in one piece, you will have to recalculate the border fabric yardages. (For instance, to cut an 88½" unpieced border, you will need a 2½ yard length of fabric.)

As mentioned on page 23, pieced tops often vary in size slightly from what has been mathe- matically planned. Border measurements for these quilts have been given based on mathematics. Especially for the large quilts, you should check the measurements of your top before cutting or applying the long border pieces, and adjust the border cutting dimensions to match your top.

For a number of reasons, including the hills and valleys created by the quilting process, completed quilts are usually slightly smaller than the dimensions planned. Finished dimensions given in this section are based, again, on mathematics. Unless it is stretched and fastened to a wall or frame, the finished quilt will probably measure slightly smaller than the dimensions listed.

The final two quilts in the book, *Monkey Wrench* and *Double T*, are much more complicated to construct. They are intended to stretch the limits of traditional quilt construction methods. These two quilts are not sewn from repeated blocks but are conceived as an overall surface design.

In working with this type of quilt design, requiring an enormous number of templates, I draw the piecing pattern for the whole quilt at full size on the gridded vellum described on page 19. Write a color designation in each piece of the full-size drawing. Colored markers can also help to keep things straight.

As explained on page 19, as the fabrics are chosen, the original vellum drawing is cut up to produce the templates, and each piece of fabric for the quilt is cut out individually. Taping the vellum pieces back together after using them helps you keep track of the assembly process.

Monkey Wrench and *Double T* are very compli- cated to put together and are recommended only for quiltmakers of considerable experience and lots of patience. It would be extremely helpful for you to construct one or more of the simpler quilts in the book first, to master the reverberant patterning process, before attempting either of these. The concept of constructing a quilt from a full-size drawing greatly expands the possibilities for making your own original designs. Drafting one of these quilts full-size is a learning experience in itself and will give you an opportunity to stretch your abilities as a quiltmaker.

In calculating yardage, all fabric is assumed to be 44–45″ wide. Yardages should be recalculated for fabrics of other widths.

MAPLE LEAF

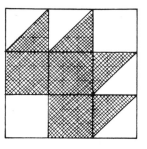

The traditional *Maple Leaf* block makes a very dynamic quilt. The block itself is simple—a nine-patch of light and dark squares and half-square triangles. I wanted to make a bold, dramatic statement with my *Maple Leaf*, so I chose bright colors and a lot of value contrast for my fabrics.

For this quilt, I utilized the very simple fact that red and blue combine to produce purple. The fabrics selected are several different reds, blues and purples of a similar value and intensity. Although I could have accomplished the same type of transparency with the choice of one red, one blue and one purple fabric, I think the quilt surface is much more interesting in the combination of several very similar fabrics of each color. The background fabric is white with a tiny blue print.

In designing the quilt, I began with 36 blocks of blue maple leaves, arranged so that each one is oriented in the same direction. The blocks are 12″ squares composed of 4″ squares and half-square triangles.

Superimposed on the thirty-six blue leaves are four 36″ blocks of red maple leaves. The red leaves point up to the left while the blue blocks point up to the right.

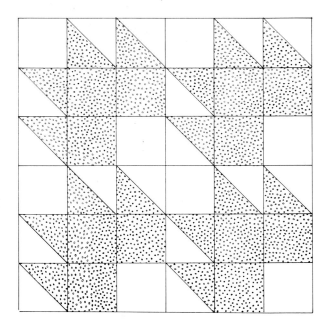

Where the blue leaves overlap the red leaves, the colored patches are purple.

Having pieced this high-chroma center, it seemed that I would have to continue to use colors of this conviction to frame the quilt. Hence the border of orange, bright pink and teal green. The sawtooth border is made from the same half-square template used in the smaller maple leaf block, a visual repetition of a design element useful in tying the border to the pieced center.

I chose to quilt an even larger scale of the *Maple Leaf* block over the surface of the quilt. Using bright blue thread and doing the quilting on the sewing machine made a dramatic statement. On the reverse side, the bright blue quilting design creates a whole-cloth quilt of hot pink with a narrow blue-green border.

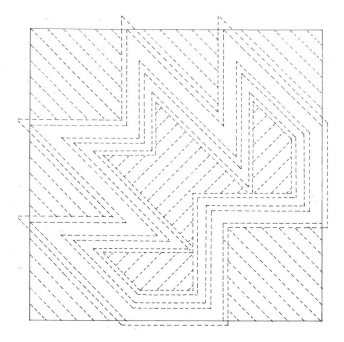

A quilting design of any of these scales of maple leaves could be produced on a commercial quilting machine. Using the type of machine that has a stylus which follows a linear quilting pattern, the maple leaves could be produced with two passes of the machine using the pattern shown here.

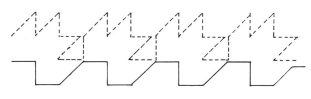

Other color combinations would work well with this design, such as pastel pink/lavender/blue with a peach, light pink and aqua border. Or the natural autumn colors of maple leaves and a red/orange/yellow transparency.

Many other scales of maple leaves could have been chosen for the quilting stitches. A simple one would put one quilted maple leaf in each 4″ block, but a quilting pattern size that does not evenly overlap the pieced design produces especially interesting patterns, too.

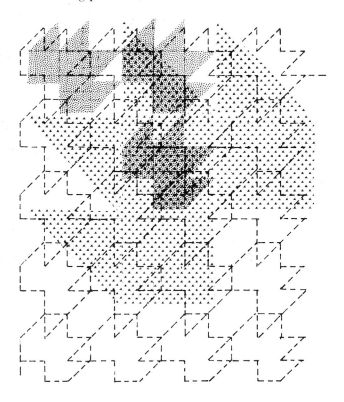

Back

To make an 88½" by 88½" quilt as illustrated here, you will need:

COLOR	TEMPLATE			TOTAL YARDAGE
	1	**2**	**3**	
A blue	40	64	32	1½
B red	40	64	32	1½
AB purple	52	80	32	1¾
Background	32	48	32	1¼
Pink (border)	—	72	—	1¼
Orange (border)	—	72	—	2¾
Outer border	Cut 2 (4½" by 80½")			
	Cut 2 (4½" by 88½")			
Teal				1
Inner border	Cut 4 (2½" by 76½")			
Corner blocks	Cut 4 (6½" by 6½")			

Backing fabric: 6½ yards, pieced

To make a 44½" by 44½" quilted wallhanging, you will need:

COLOR	TEMPLATE			TOTAL YARDAGE
	4	**5**	**6**	
A blue	40	64	32	½
B red	40	64	32	⅝
AB purple	52	80	32	¾
Background	32	48	32	½
Pink (border)	—	72	—	⅜
Orange (border)	—	72	—	1½
Outer borders	Cut 2 (2½" x 40½")			
	Cut 2 (2½" x 44½")			
Teal				¼
Inner borders	Cut 4 (1½" by 38½")			
Corner blocks	Cut 4 (3½" by 3½")			

Backing fabric: 2⅝ yards of 45" wide

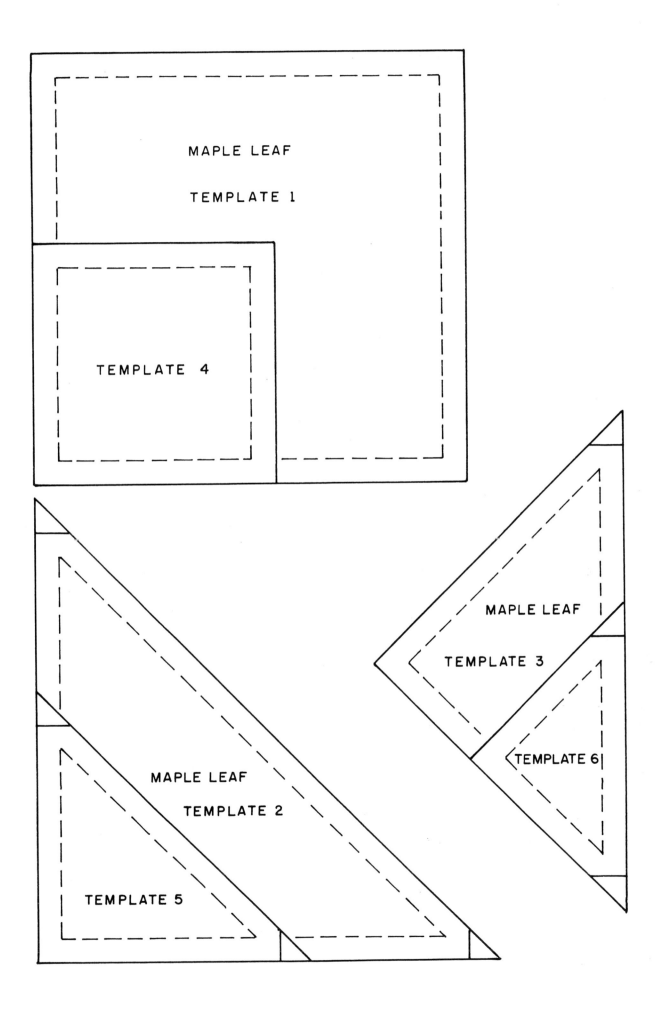

MILL WHEEL

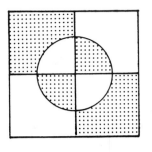

There are several possible arrangements for the *Mill Wheel* block. The repeating geometry is a quarter circle, drawn here with a 3½″ radius at one corner of a 6″ square. Four of these 6″ squares are put together to make the *Mill Wheel* block, with the colors alternated.

I have made two versions of the *Mill Wheel* pattern using a blue-yellow-red transparency. Although both quilts are based on the same block and finish 36″ square, one uses six templates and the other twenty-three.

Mill Wheel I begins as a blue (Color A) and white six-inch grid with a 3½″ radius circle.

A second pattern of a single *Mill Wheel* block 24″ across with a 7″ radius circle is colored red-orange (Color B) and yellow (Color C).

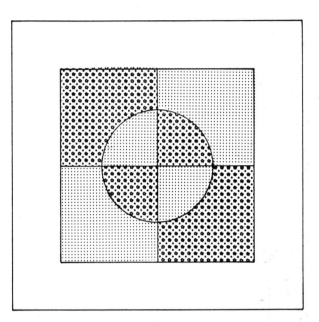

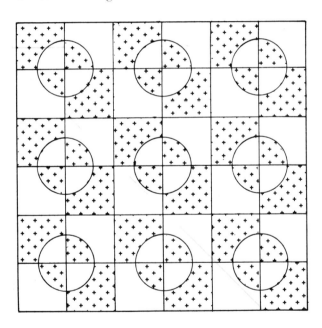

Treated as a strict transparency, when these two scales of pattern overlap, red over blue is shown as purple (Color AB) and yellow over blue is green (Color AC).

An 80% cotton-20% polyester batting has been used in *Mill Wheel I*. It is machine quilted with orange thread with the words MILL WHEEL repeated over and over in a programmed outline alphabet stitch pattern.

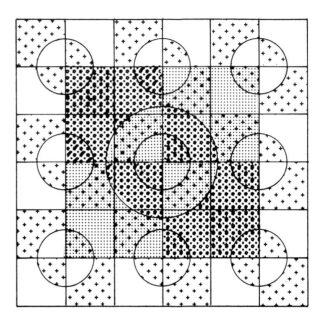

To make a 36″ by 36″ wallhanging as illustrated, you will need:

COLOR	TEMPLATE								TOTAL YARDAGE
	1	**2**	**3**	**4**	**4R**	**5**	**6**	**6R**	
A blue	10	10	—	—	—	—	—	—	½
B red	—	2	2	—	—	—	2	2	⅜
C yellow	2	6	—	2	2	2	—	—	¼
AC green	—	2	2	—	—	—	2	2	¼
AB purple	2	6	—	2	2	2	—	—	¼
white	10	10	—	—	—	—	—	—	½

Backing fabric: 1⅛ yards of 45″ wide

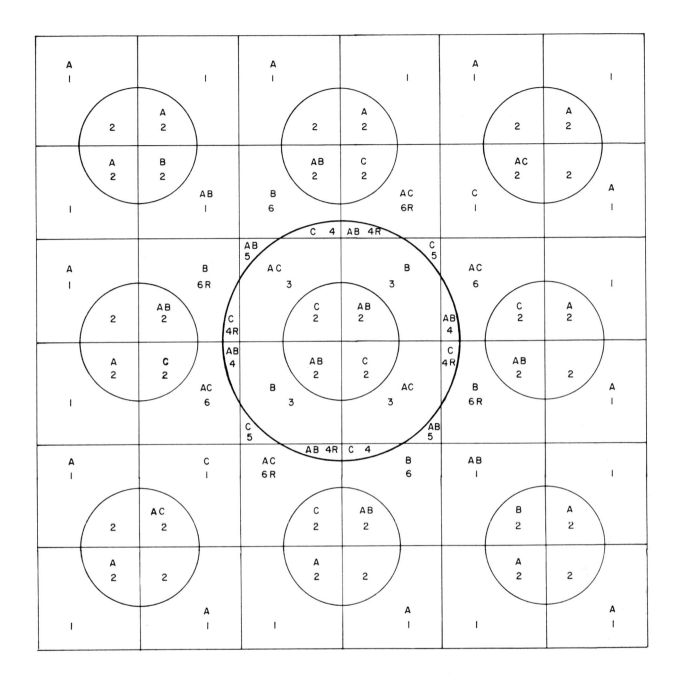

Mill Wheel II

Mill Wheel II, a second version of the same pattern, begins with the same blue and white grid.

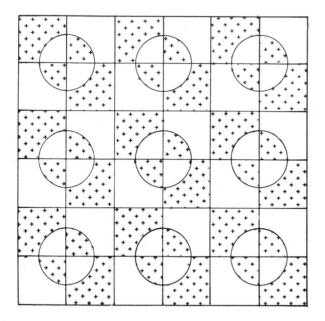

This time the larger scale of pattern, with a half-block repeat, is drawn at an angle.

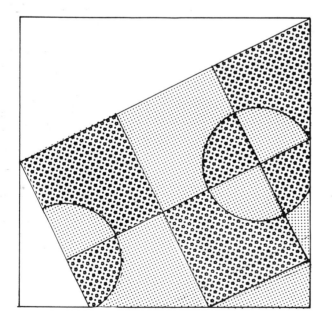

The specific angle was chosen so that some of the intersections of the grid of the larger pattern would fall on intersections of the smaller pattern, in order to make construction somewhat easier and to cut down on the number of templates required.

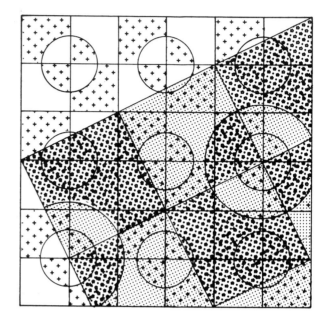

The overlapped pattern is again a blue-yellow-red transparency, although with some slightly different fabric choices. This time, because of the skewed grids, twenty-three templates are needed.

45   MILL WHEEL

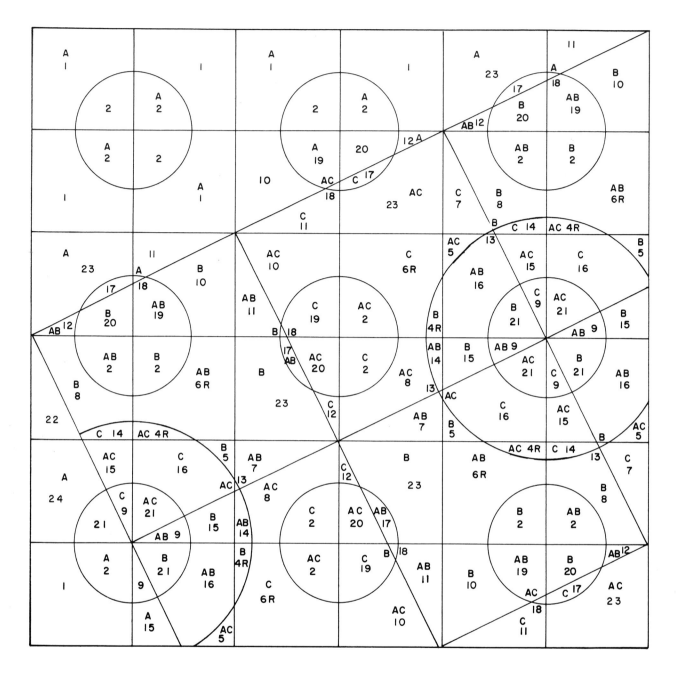

Mill Wheel II is assembled with an 80% cotton-20% polyester batting and quilted on the machine. The blue and white pattern is outlined with blue thread; the red and yellow pattern is defined by outline letters in yellow and orange thread.

To make a 36″ by 36″ wallhanging as illustrated here, you will need:

TEMPLATE   **COLOR**

	A blue	B red	C yellow	AB purple	AC green	white
1	3	—	—	—	—	4
2	4	3	2	3	2	3
4R	—	2	—	—	3	—
5	—	3	—	—	3	—
6R	—	—	2	3	—	—
7	—	—	2	2	—	—
8	—	3	—	—	2	—
9	—	—	3	3	—	1
10	—	3	—	—	2	1
11	—	—	2	2	—	2
12	1	—	2	3	—	—
13	—	2	—	—	2	—
14	—	—	3	2	—	—
15	1	3	—	—	3	—
16	—	—	3	3	—	—
17	—	—	2	2	—	2
18	2	2	—	—	2	—
19	1	—	2	3	—	—
20	—	3	—	—	2	1
21	—	3	—	—	3	1
22	—	—	—	—	—	1
23	2	2	—	—	2	—
24	1	—	—	—	—	—

YARDAGE

A blue	B red	C yellow	AB purple	AC green	white
⅜	½	½	½	½	⅜

Backing fabric: 1⅛ yards of 45″ wide

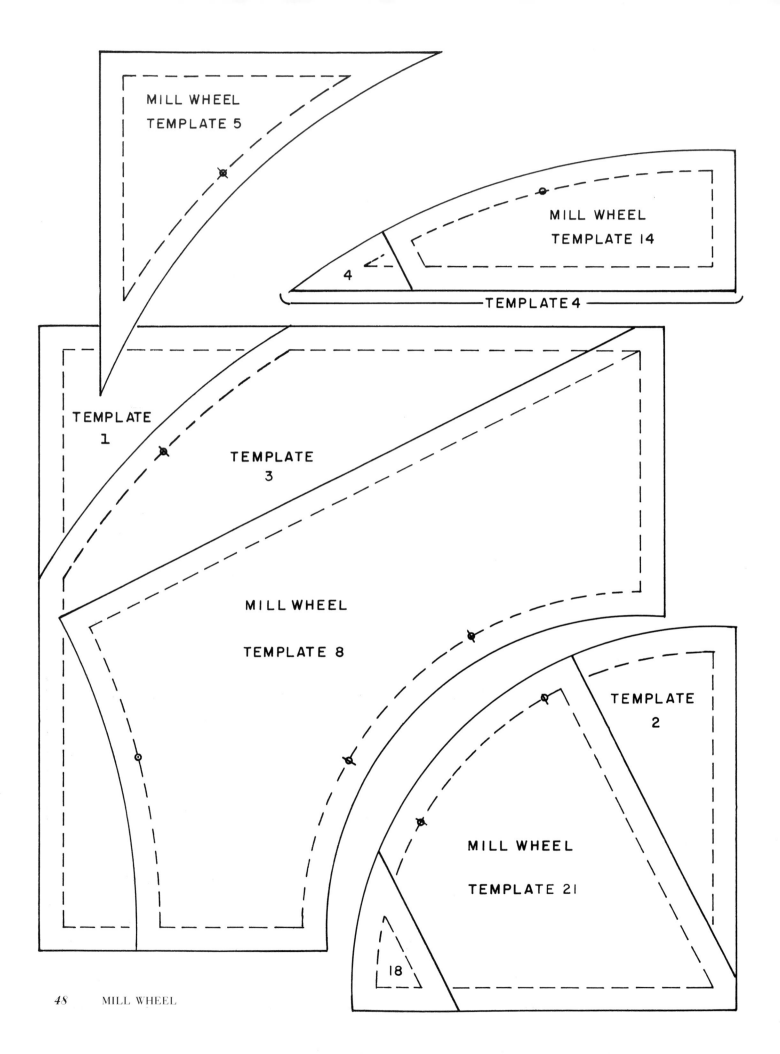

MILL WHEEL
TEMPLATE 5

MILL WHEEL
TEMPLATE 14

4

TEMPLATE 4

TEMPLATE 1

TEMPLATE 3

MILL WHEEL

TEMPLATE 8

TEMPLATE 2

MILL WHEEL

TEMPLATE 21

18

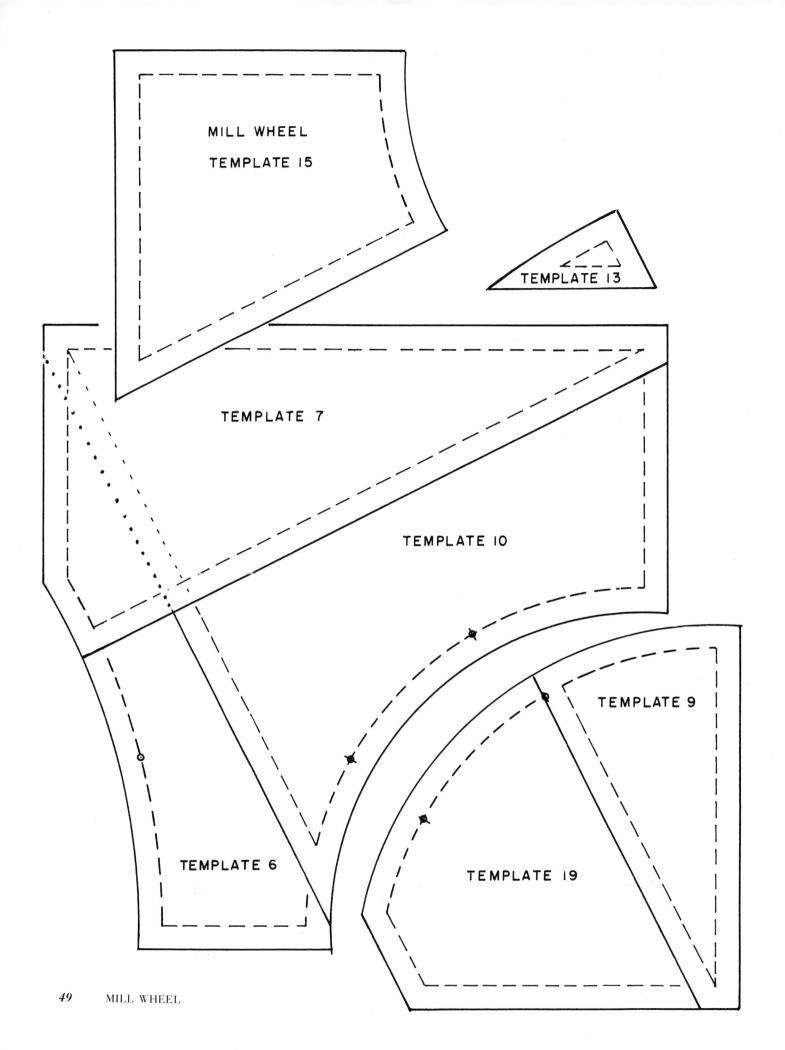

MILL WHEEL

TEMPLATE 15

TEMPLATE 13

TEMPLATE 7

TEMPLATE 10

TEMPLATE 9

TEMPLATE 6

TEMPLATE 19

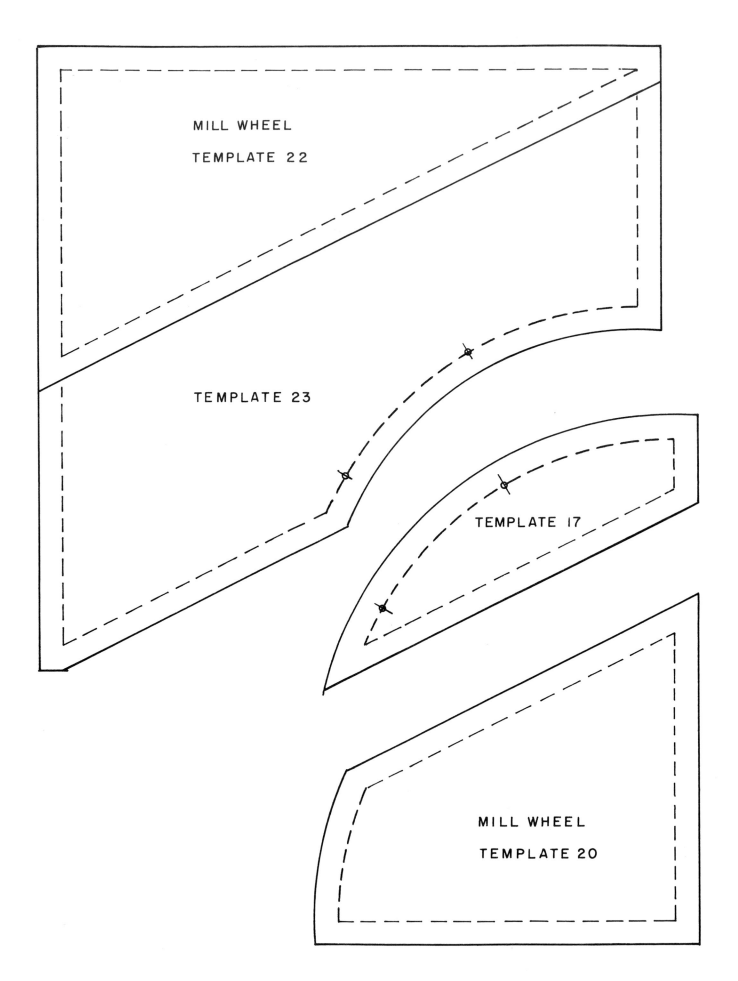

MILL WHEEL

TEMPLATE 22

TEMPLATE 23

TEMPLATE 17

MILL WHEEL

TEMPLATE 20

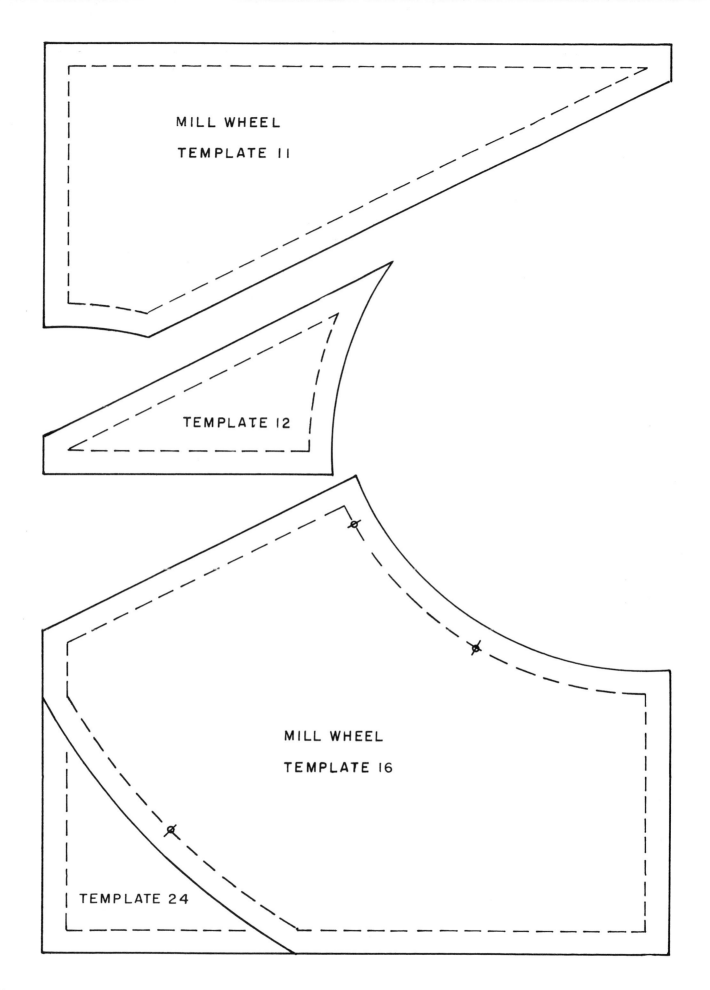

MILL WHEEL

TEMPLATE 11

TEMPLATE 12

MILL WHEEL

TEMPLATE 16

TEMPLATE 24

BIRDS IN THE AIR

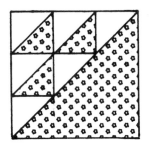

In trying to think of straightforward ways of demonstrating transparency effects with fabric, I happened on a group of co-ordinated fabrics at a shop. The transparency works perfectly. The same pattern is printed in two colorways: the black-and-white and the navy-and-blue fabrics. As used in this quilt, they give the effect of a clear blue film placed in triangular sections over a quilt of black and white fabric.

The size of the *Birds in the Air* block was chosen to complement this particular fabric. Template 1 is 3″ on a side and forms a major design element. Template 4 is 9″. After experiments with paper windows cut with various sizes of right triangles, these two seemed to work best with the scale of pattern in the fabric.

I began the design with thirty-six 9″ blocks, all oriented in the same direction.

Four 36″ blocks were arranged in the opposite direction.

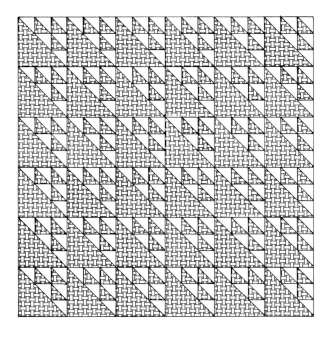

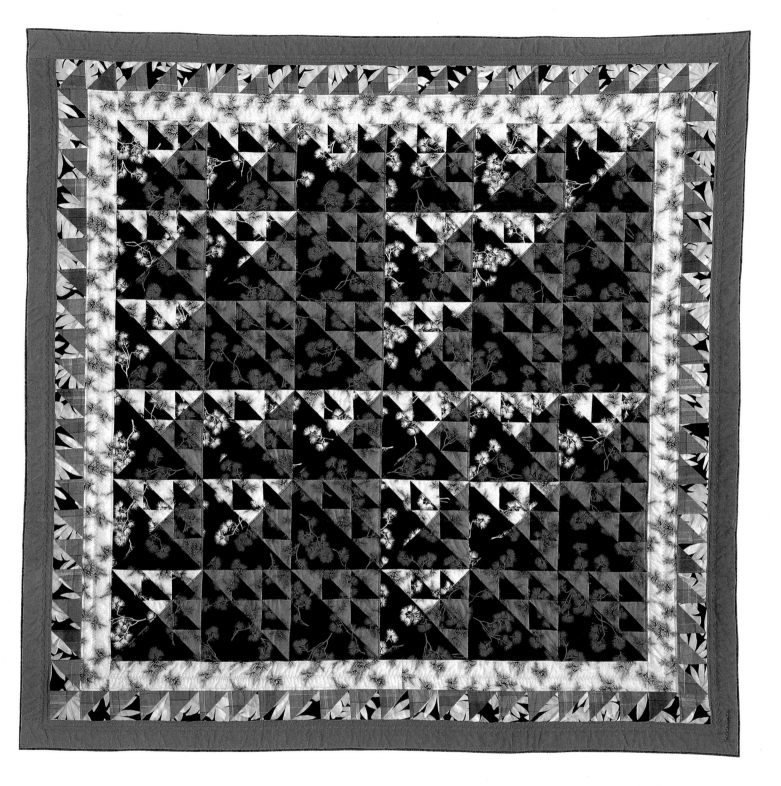

The mustard yellow Madras plaid that I used in the border of this quilt is a nice companion to the blues. I find the colors in Madras plaids very useful, as they seem to be designed with a different color sense from most commercial American fabrics. This mustard yellow is especially hard to find in quilt fabric (Color E).

The other fabric used with the mustard in the sawtooth border is a large-scale black/white/buff print, from a one-yard remnant I found especially attractive. As I was piecing the blue and black blocks for *Birds in the Air*, this fabric was lying on the floor nearby because I hadn't yet gotten around to putting it away. My eyes kept going back and forth between this fabric and the quilt forming on the design wall. It's perhaps not a choice of fabric that I would have thought up out of thin air, but I believe it works perfectly.

The outer 3″ lavender border (Color G) makes an effective finishing edge to the quilt, picking up a bit of lavender in the mustard plaid.

The back of the quilt is a *Nine Patch* of 19½″ blocks, surrounded by a 5″ border of the white print and an outer border of the plaid. The outer

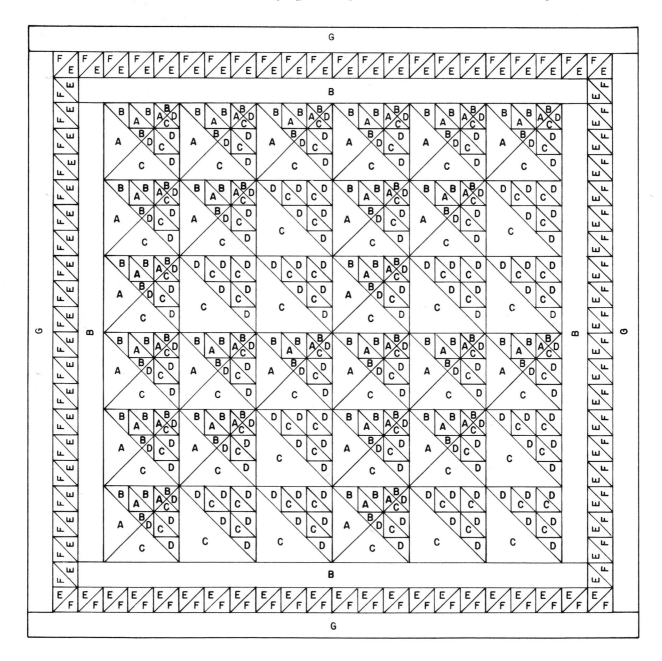

Back

dimensions of the *Nine Patch* were intentionally not to match any of the piecing on the front of the quilt. The edge of the *Nine Patch* falls somewhere within the white print border on the front of the quilt. Matching seams exactly on the front and back of a two-sided quilt is almost impossible. I prefer to avoid that problem by designing around it.

The extra seams in a pieced back are not troublesome when the piece is to be machine quilted, although care should probably be taken in assembling the quilt sandwich to keep the layers squared up.

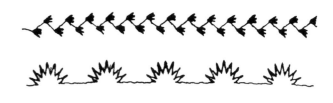

The quilting was done on the machine with navy cotton thread in the center blocks, off-white in the white border, and gray in the lavender border. The quilting was done from the front with a straight stitch and an even-feed foot ¼" from the seam lines. A row of fancy stitching fastens the white print border and the lavender band.

For this quilt, which is 72½" by 72½", you will need:

COLOR	TEMPLATE				TOTAL YARDAGE
	1	2	3	4	
A (black print)	24	—	24	24	2
B (white print)	48	—	48	—	2½
C (navy print)	60	12	24	24	2
D (blue print)	120	—	48	—	2
E (mustard plaid)	84	—	—	—	1½
F (black/white/buff)	84	—	—	—	½
G (lavender solid)	—	—	—	—	1

White print front borders	cut 2 (54½" by 3½")
Color B	cut 2 (60½" by 3½")
Lavender solid front borders	cut 2 (66½" by 3½")
Color G	cut 2 (72½" by 3½")
White print back borders	cut 2 (59" by 5½")
Color B	cut 2 (69½" by 5½")
Mustard plaid back borders	cut 2 (69½" by 4")
Color E	cut 2 (77½" by 4")
Nine-patch on back	4 Color A Black print
20" by 20" squares	1 Color C Navy print
(cut size)	4 Color D Blue print

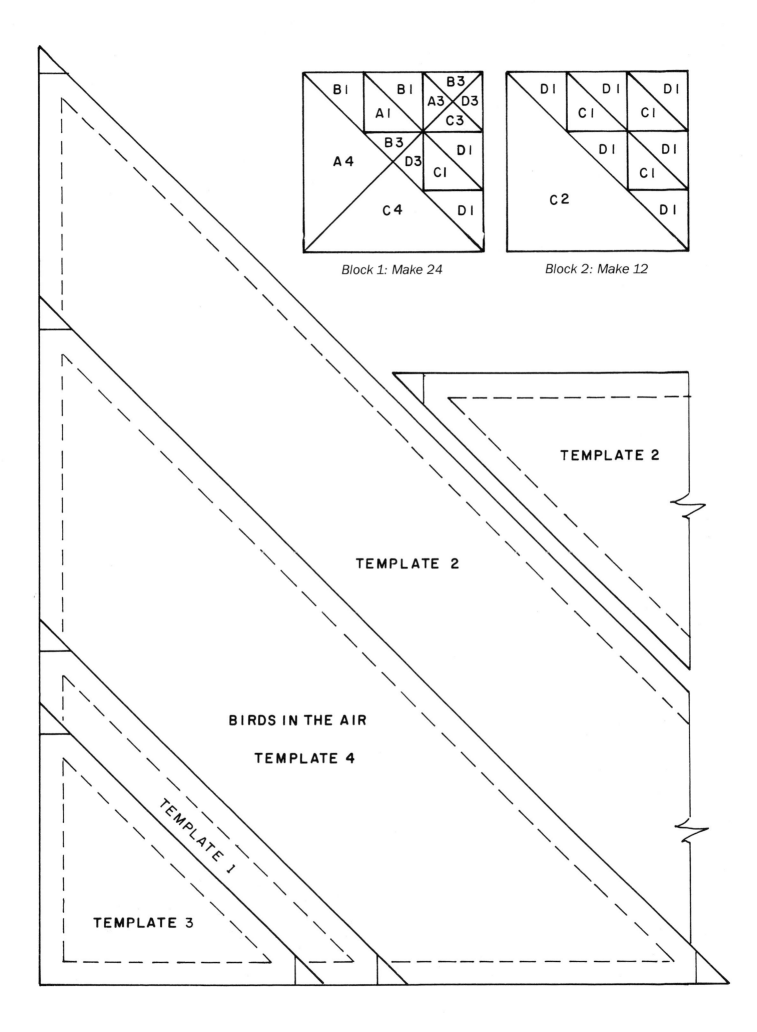

			B3
B1	B1	A3	D3
	A1		C3
A4	B3		D1
	D3	C1	
	C4		D1

Block 1: Make 24

D1	D1	D1
C1	C1	
D1	D1	
C2	C1	D1

Block 2: Make 12

TEMPLATE 2

TEMPLATE 2

BIRDS IN THE AIR

TEMPLATE 4

TEMPLATE 1

TEMPLATE 3

FIRE ON THE MOUNTAIN

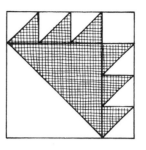

The pattern used here is a very slight modification of the traditional *Delectable Mountains* block. Unlike the previous quilts, it is assembled

as a linear band of pattern rather than as separate square blocks.

My *Fire on the Mountain* quilt is made with a red/orange/yellow transparency. Neutral grays, gray/brown, grayed lavenders and blue-greens were used in the background of the pattern, pro-

ducing a quilt that is predominantly of middle values. Many other color schemes are certainly possible. A good one might be to color the moun- tains differently from the little flames on their sides.

The quilt was assembled in horizontal rows.

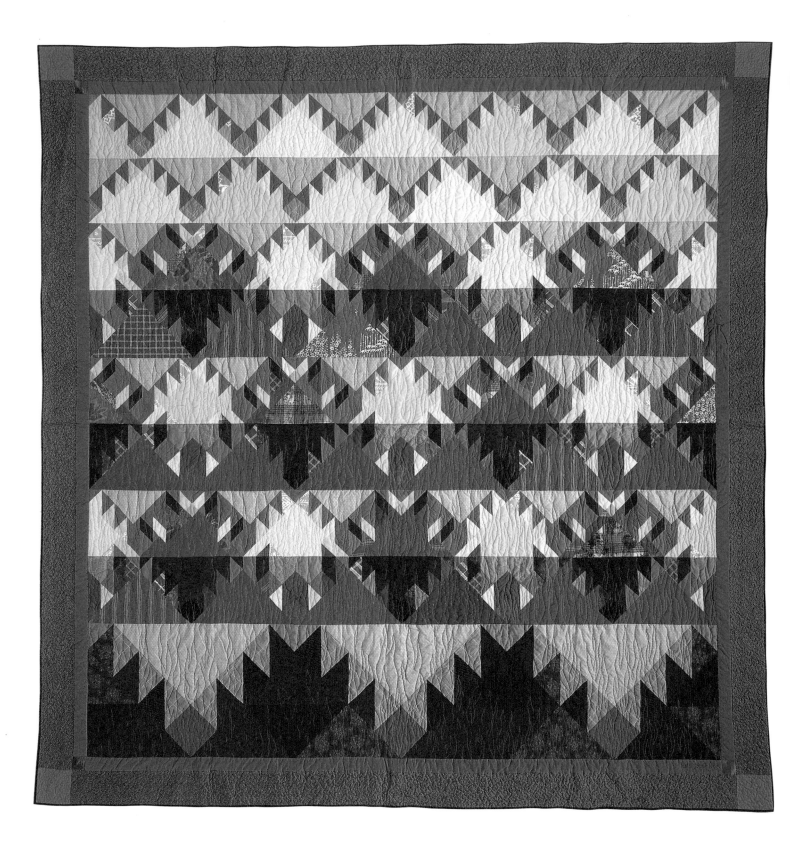

When the two patterns are overlapped, the smaller pattern in yellow appears alone at the top of the quilt. The larger pattern in red appears alone at the bottom. On the central six bands, the red and yellow patterns overlap and are pieced of oranges and red-oranges, but with little bits of yellow and red remaining where the patterns do not overlap completely.

The border for this fiery quilt is composed of a 2″ band of lavender with blue print corner blocks and an outer border of ashes. The ashes are made from a tiny gray-black-and-white calico, a very different visual texture from the other fabrics in the quilt. Dusty lavender corner blocks complete the outer border. A ½″ binding of a small-scale charcoal gray drapery print finishes the edge. The quilt pictured here has a finished size of 110½″ by 114½″, large enough for a king-size bed. By drafting the pattern to a smaller scale, or decreasing the number of repeats, you can construct other sizes.

Quilting this piece on the home sewing machine, while mechanically difficult, was lots of fun. Practically speaking, in quilting a large piece such as *Fire on the Mountain*, free-motion quilting is constrained by the mechanical difficulty of handling large pieces under the arm of the machine and by having to stop to reposition your hands every few inches. Commercial quilting machines solve some of these difficulties. It would have been significantly easier to have handled this piece as quilt-as-you-go in horizontal rows. All of the quilting was done by eye, without first marking the quilting lines with pencil.

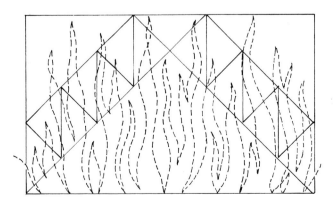

Fire on the Mountain is free-motion machine quilted in patterns of flames, worked in horizontal bands. Pale aqua 50-weight cotton thread was used as a top thread and lavender or orange or yellow or red thread on the bobbin in each horizontal row. The large fiery mountains at the bottom are quilted in leaping flames with orange or yellow thread on the top spool.

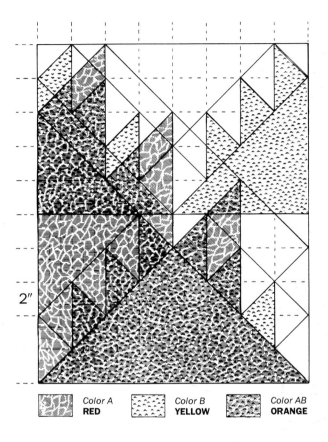

2″

| Color A **RED** | Color B **YELLOW** | Color AB **ORANGE** |

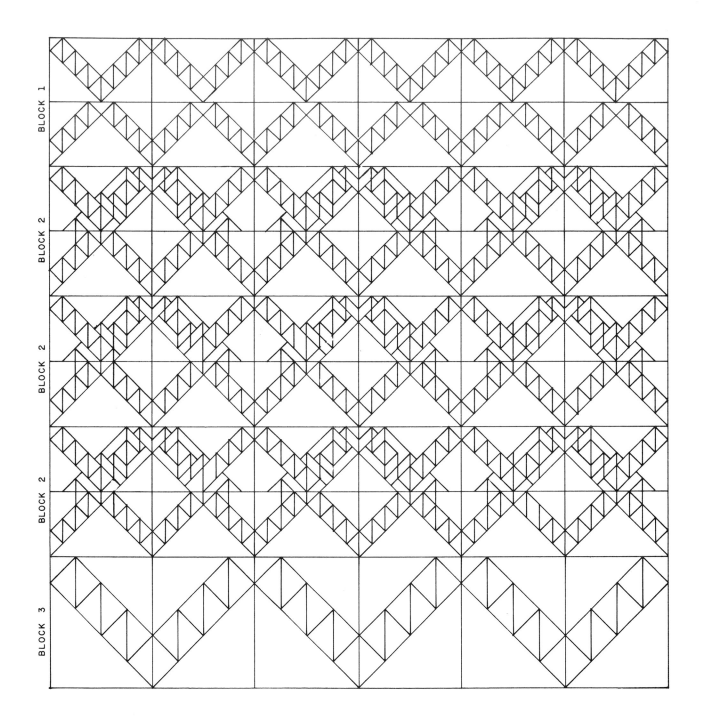

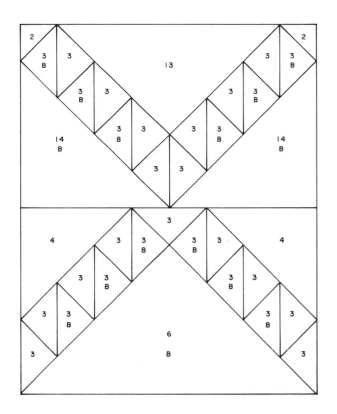

Make 6

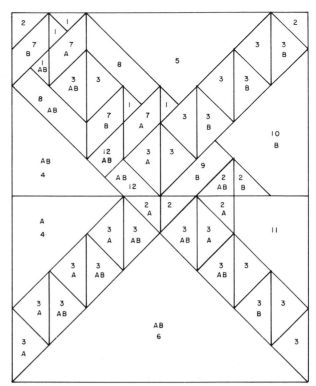

Make 9 blocks and 9 reversed blocks

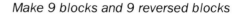

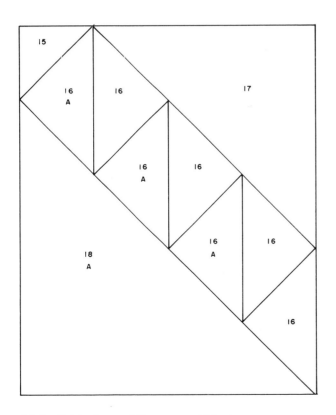

Make 3 blocks and 3 reversed blocks

To make a 110½″ by 114½″ quilt as illustrated here, you will need:

TEMPLATE   **COLOR**

	A (red)	B (yellow)	AB (orange)	Background
1	—	—	18	72
2	36	18	18	66
3	108	144	108	246
4	18	—	18	12
5	—	—	—	18
6	—	6	18	—
7	18	18	—	—
7R	18	18	—	—
8	—	—	9	9
8R	—	—	9	9
9	—	9	—	—
9R	—	9	—	—
10	—	9	—	—
10R	—	9	—	—
11	—	—	—	9
11R	—	—	—	9
12	—	—	36	—
13	—	—	—	6
14	—	12	—	—
15	—	—	—	6
16	18	—	—	24
17	—	—	—	6
18	6	—	—	—
Total Yardage	3¼	1¾	3	4¾

I used several different oranges, yellows and reds for Colors A, B and AB, rather than a single fabric for each.

Lavender inner border: 2½ yds.

      Cut 2 (2½″ by 96½″)   (You will have to

      Cut 2 (2½″ by 100½″)   piece these.)

Blue print corner blocks:

      Cut 4 (2½″ by 2½″) from scrap

Ashes outer border: 2½ yds.

      Cut 2 (5½″ by 100½″)   (You will have to

      Cut 2 (5½″ by 104½″)   piece these.)

Dusty lavender corner blocks: ¼ yd.

      Cut 4 (5½″ by 5½″)

Backing: 9½ yds.

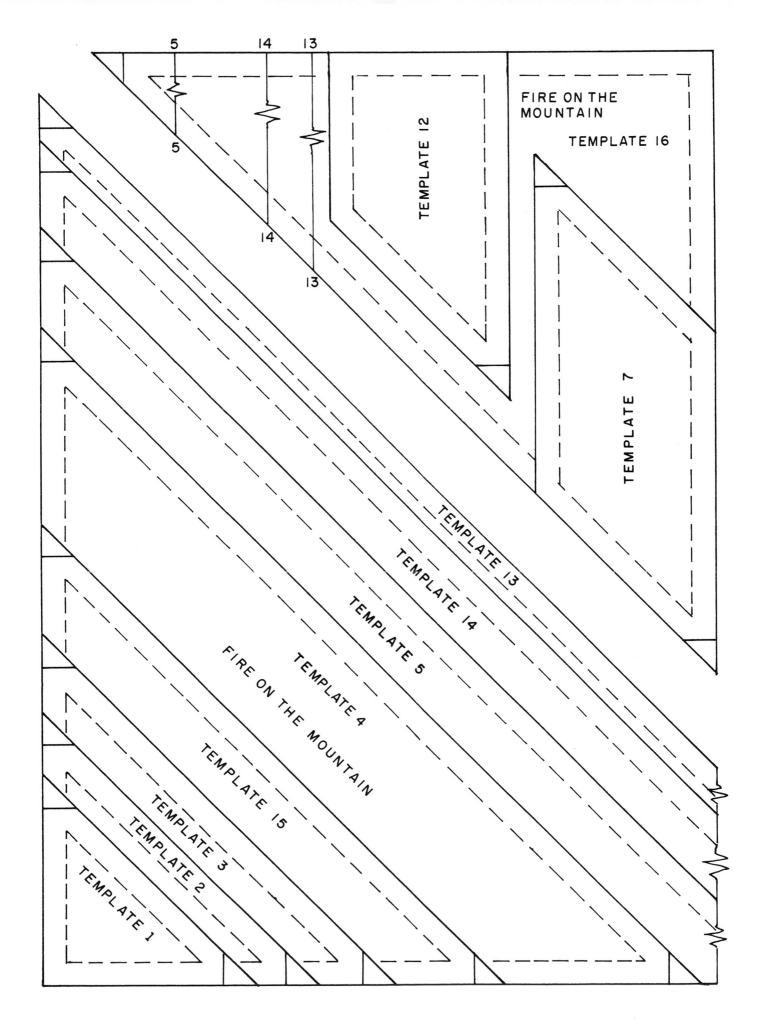

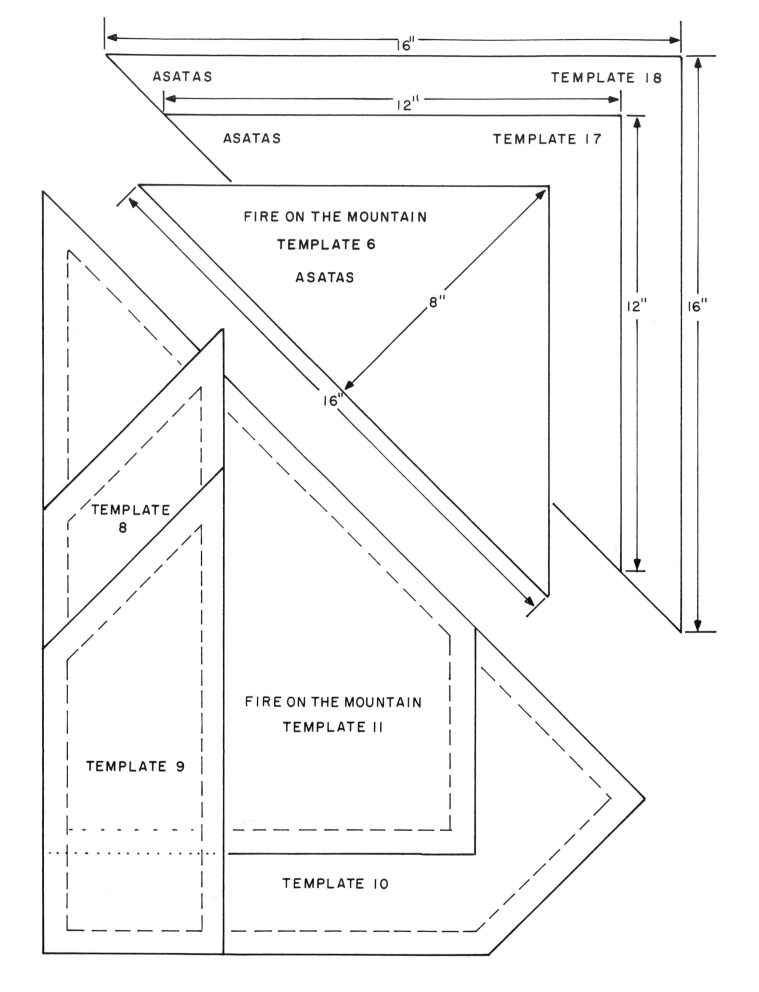

16"

ASATAS

TEMPLATE 18

12"

ASATAS

TEMPLATE 17

FIRE ON THE MOUNTAIN

TEMPLATE 6

ASATAS

8"

12"

16"

16"

TEMPLATE
8

TEMPLATE 9

FIRE ON THE MOUNTAIN

TEMPLATE 11

TEMPLATE 10

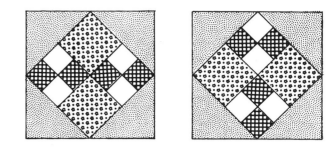

FOUR PATCH VARIATION

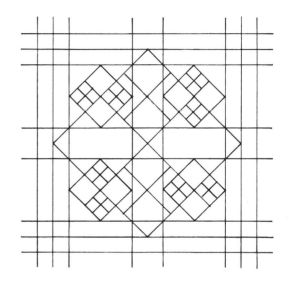

A *Four Patch* is one of the simplest quilt blocks, composed of four identical squares and usually colored with alternate lights and darks. A traditional variation incorporates two small four-patches within a larger four-patch set on point within a square. I made a further variation by turning one of the little four-patches a quarter turn.

My intention for this quilt was to experiment with a traditional block set together with sashing as the base pattern from which the reverberant design evolved.

The initial block is 8″ on a side and is set together with a solid-color sashing strip 4″ wide. A larger scale pattern was drawn with 24″ blocks and 12″ sashing.

This larger scale of pattern will repeat evenly with the smaller. The resulting overlapped pattern is rather complex.

I decided to eliminate some of the lines to simplify the design, add a few seams to simplify the piecing, and select colors with little attempt at transparency.

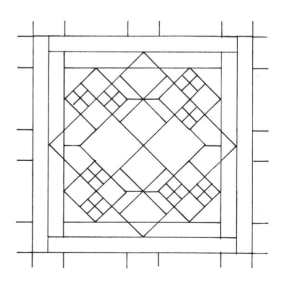

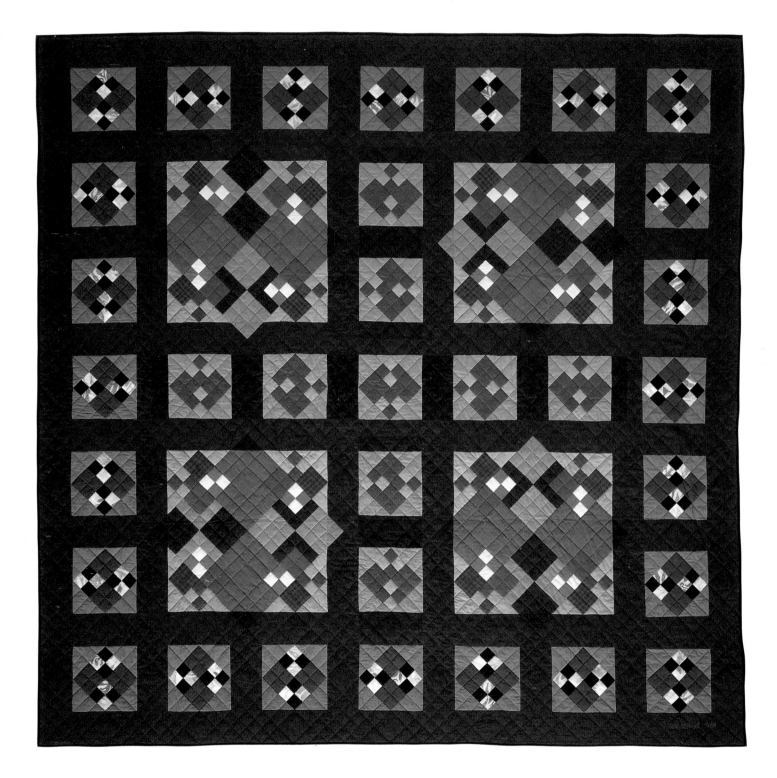

The result is a quilt with four large areas of overlapped design, sashed and bordered by bands of the smaller block.

In this *Four Patch* variation, the pattern for the quilting stitches is an interrupted grid, stitched in the ditch along lines set up by the pieced pattern. I used smoke-colored transparent nylon thread (gray on the bobbin) with an even-feed foot.

As constructed, with 8″ blocks and 4″ sashing, the *Four Patch* variation finishes 88½″ square. The little four-patches can be sewn by traditional methods (four squares cut separately or stack cut in quantity and pieced together) or by one of the quick-piecing strip methods (see page 19).

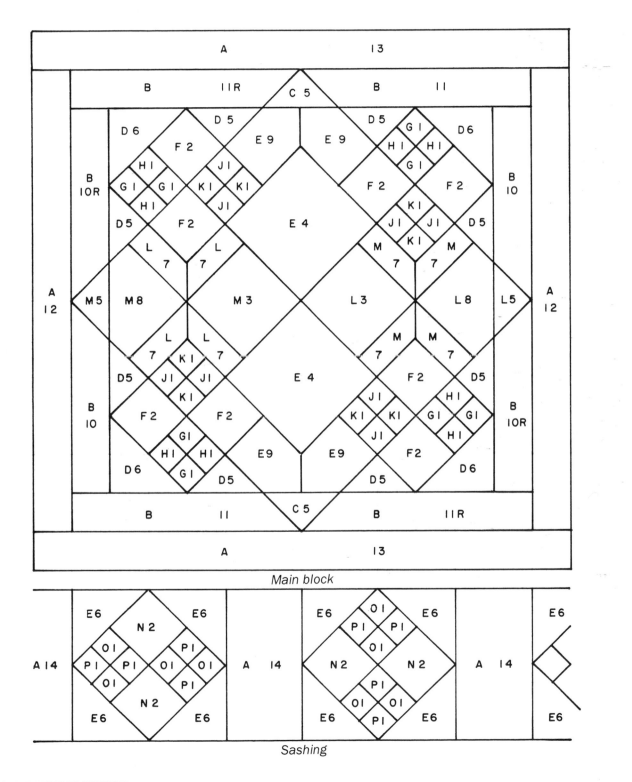

Main block

Sashing

To make an 88½″ by 88½″ quilt as illustrated here, you will need:

COLOR											TEMPLATE						
	1	2	3	4	5	6	7	7R	8	9	10	10R	11	11R	12	13	14
A	—	—	—	—	—	—	—	—	—	—	—	—	—	—	8	8	—
B	—	—	—	—	—	—	—	—	—	—	8	8	8	8	—	—	—
C	—	—	—	—	8	—	—	—	—	—	—	—	—	—	—	—	—
D	—	—	—	—	32	16	—	—	—	—	—	—	—	—	—	—	—
E	—	—	—	8	—	—	—	—	—	16	—	—	—	—	—	—	—
F	—	32	—	—	—	—	—	—	—	—	—	—	—	—	—	—	—
G	32	—	—	—	—	—	—	—	—	—	—	—	—	—	—	—	—
H	32	—	—	—	—	—	—	—	—	—	—	—	—	—	—	—	—
J	32	—	—	—	—	—	—	—	—	—	—	—	—	—	—	—	—
K	32	—	—	—	—	—	—	—	—	—	—	—	—	—	—	—	—
L	—	—	4	—	—	—	8	8	4	—	—	—	—	—	—	—	—
M	—	—	4	—	—	—	8	8	4	—	—	—	—	—	—	—	—

Sashing

	1	2	3	4	5	6	7	7R	8	9	10	10R	11	11R	12	13	14
F	—	18	—	—	—	—	—	—	—	—	—	—	—	—	—	—	—
G	36	—	—	—	—	—	—	—	—	—	—	—	—	—	—	—	—
H	36	—	—	—	—	—	—	—	—	—	—	—	—	—	—	—	—
E	—	—	—	—	—	36	—	—	—	—	—	—	—	—	—	—	—
A	—	—	—	—	—	—	—	—	—	—	—	—	—	—	—	—	12

Outer border

	1	2	3	4	5	6	7	7R	8	9	10	10R	11	11R	12	13	14
N	—	48	—	—	—	—	—	—	—	—	—	—	—	—	—	—	—
O	96	—	—	—	—	—	—	—	—	—	—	—	—	—	—	—	—
P	96	—	—	—	—	—	—	—	—	—	—	—	—	—	—	—	—
E	—	—	—	—	—	96	—	—	—	—	—	—	—	—	—	—	—
A	—	—	—	—	—	—	—	—	—	—	—	—	—	—	—	—	24
A	Cut 2 (4½″ by 80½″)
A	Cut 2 (4½″ by 88½″)

COLOR		TOTAL YARDAGE
A	red/brown	3
B	claret	3/8
C	blue/purple	1/8
D	lavender	3/8
E	teal	2¼
F	red	5/8
G	dark green	¼
H	light green	¼
J	green	¼
K	yellow	¼
L	peach	3/8
M	navy	3/8
N	purple	1
O	black/green	3/8
P	pink	3/8

Backing fabric: 6 yards of 50″-60″ wide fabric or 7½ yards of 36″-45″ wide fabric

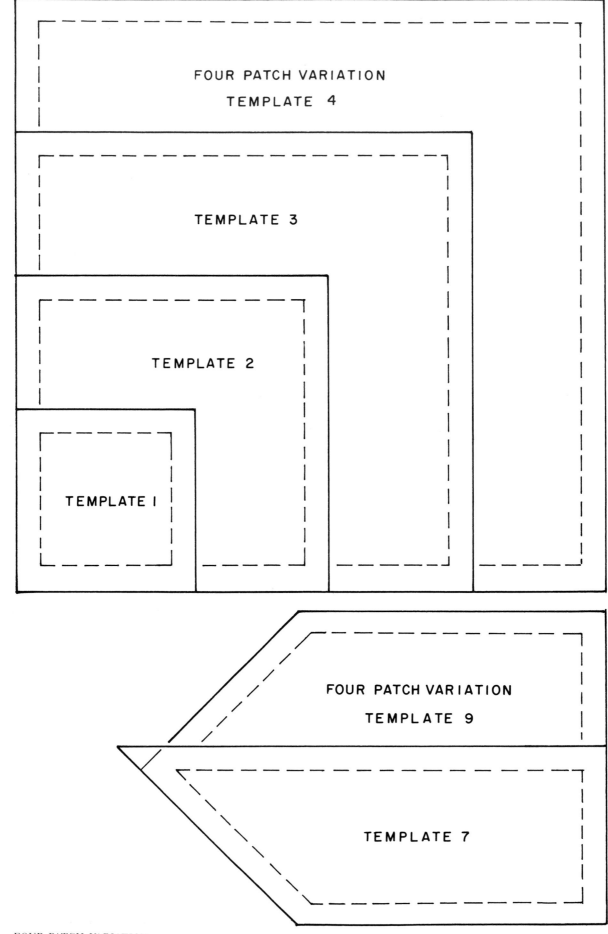

FOUR PATCH VARIATION

TEMPLATE 4

TEMPLATE 3

TEMPLATE 2

TEMPLATE 1

FOUR PATCH VARIATION

TEMPLATE 9

TEMPLATE 7

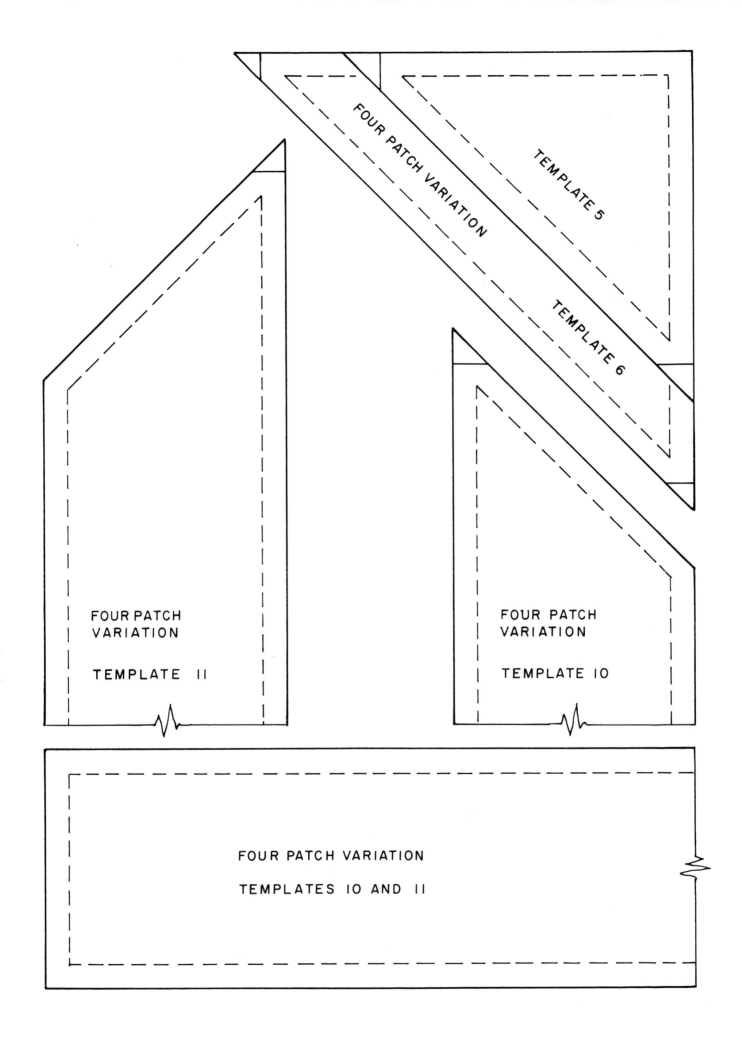

TEMPLATE 5

FOUR PATCH VARIATION

TEMPLATE 6

FOUR PATCH
VARIATION

TEMPLATE 11

FOUR PATCH
VARIATION

TEMPLATE 10

FOUR PATCH VARIATION

TEMPLATES 10 AND 11

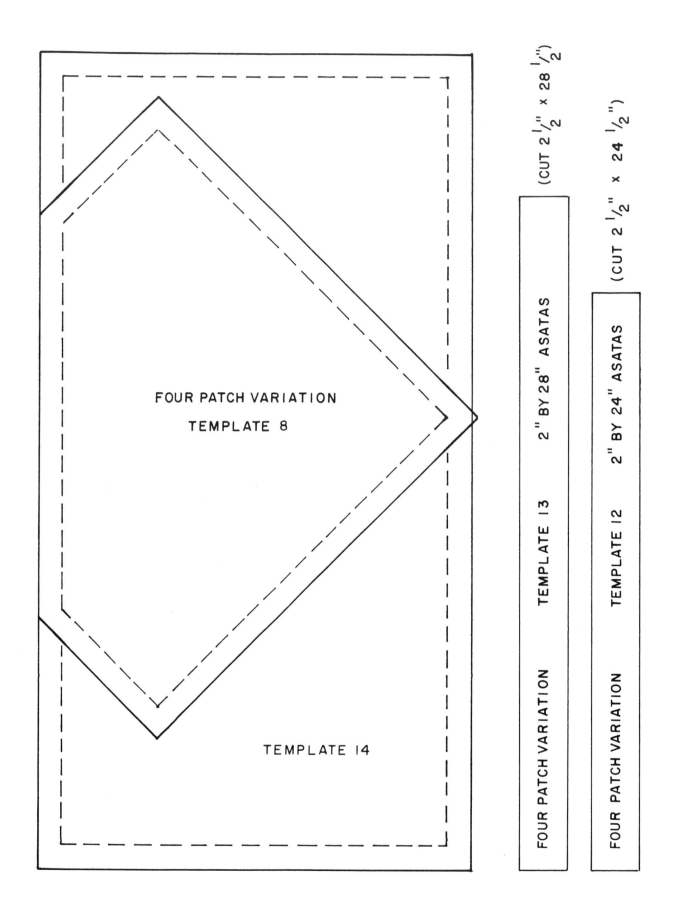

FOUR PATCH VARIATION

TEMPLATE 8

TEMPLATE 14

TEMPLATE 13   2" BY 28" ASATAS   (CUT $2\frac{1}{2}$" × $28\frac{1}{2}$")

FOUR PATCH VARIATION

TEMPLATE 12   2" BY 24" ASATAS   (CUT $2\frac{1}{2}$" × $24\frac{1}{2}$")

FOUR PATCH VARIATION

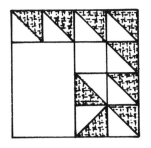

MERRY-GO-ROUND

Merry-go-round is a traditional block composed of nine colored triangles, a square and a rectangle.

For my long, narrow wallhanging (88½" by 24½"), I began with four 8" blocks with red-purple as Color A. The four blocks form a larger 16" square, with each of the four oriented in the same direction.

Superimposed over these four blocks is one 16" block with blue triangles (Color B). Where the red-purple triangles overlap the larger blue triangles, a dark purple is used (Color AB). The dark purple is really a little too dark in value to make the transparency work perfectly. In an ideal world, you could always find a fabric that exactly suits your needs.

All of the background pieces for the center of the quilt are cut from a large-scale commercial fabric dyed in white spots on gray, green, blue and purple. I cut the background fabric into the necessary pieces without regard to the print. After the background pieces were cut, I played with their

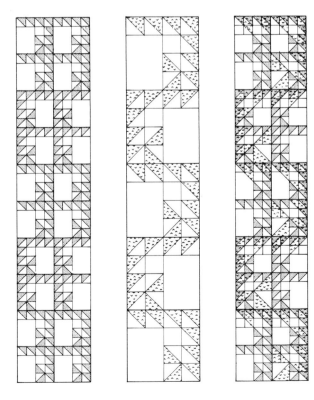

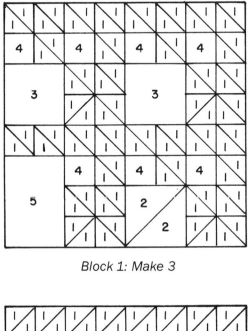

Block 1: Make 3

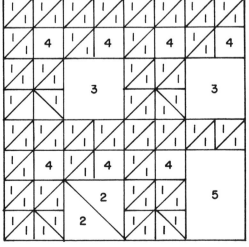

Block 1 reversed: Make 2

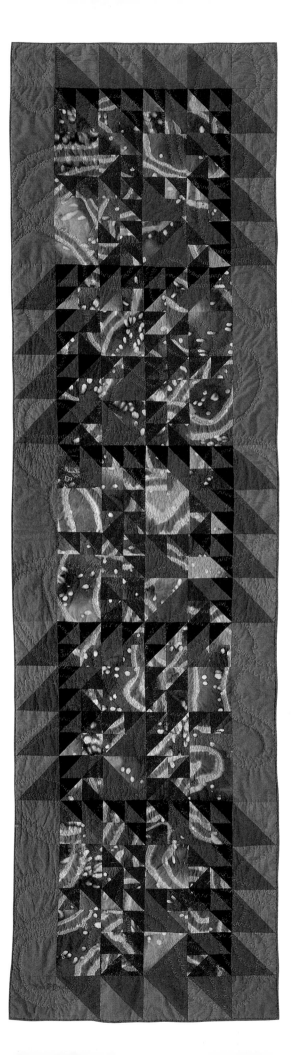

arrangement on the design wall until the resultant pattern satisfied me.

The quilt is composed of five 16″ blocks of the overlapped design, the first, third and fifth being the block as originally designed, and the second and fourth being the same block mirrored. The back and forth motion of the pieced blocks echoes the meander design dyed into the large-scale background print.

I didn't have enough of any one green to do the whole border. The variations are more interesting, anyway. In the border, three similar greens are interrupted with blue triangles (Color B) cut with Template 2.

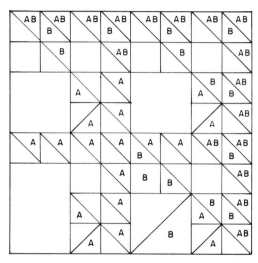

Block 1: Make 3

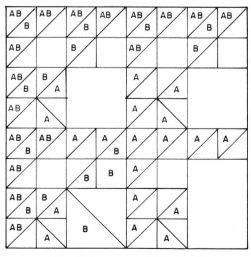

Block 1 reversed: Make 2

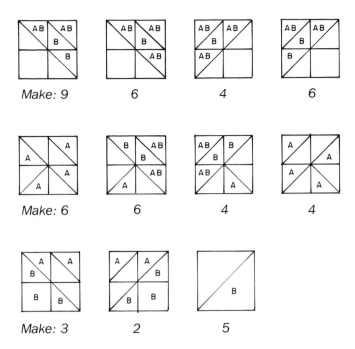

Make: 9   6   4   6

Make: 6   6   4   4

Make: 3   2   5

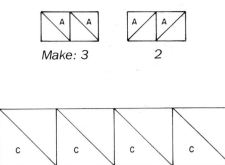

Make: 3   2

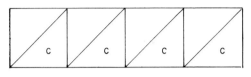

Border: Make 4

Border: Make 3

Merry-go-round was quilted using a feed-dog cover plate and darning foot in a free-motion meander pattern. The quilted meander connects the white-green-white meandering lines in the pieces of the background print, Light gray cotton size 50 sewing thread was used.

To make an 88½″ by 24½″ wallhanging as illustrated here, you will need:

TEMPLATE

	Color A	Color B	Color AB	Background
1	95	65	85	145
2	—	5	—	5
3	—	—	—	10
4	—	5	—	30
5	—	—	—	5

For the border:

	Color A	Color B	Color AB	Background
2	—	28	—	28
3	—	—	—	4
16½″ by 4½″ (cut size)	—	—	—	5

Yardage	⅜	⅝	⅜	1 (blocks)
				¾ (border)

Backing fabric: 2⅝ yards of 45″ wide

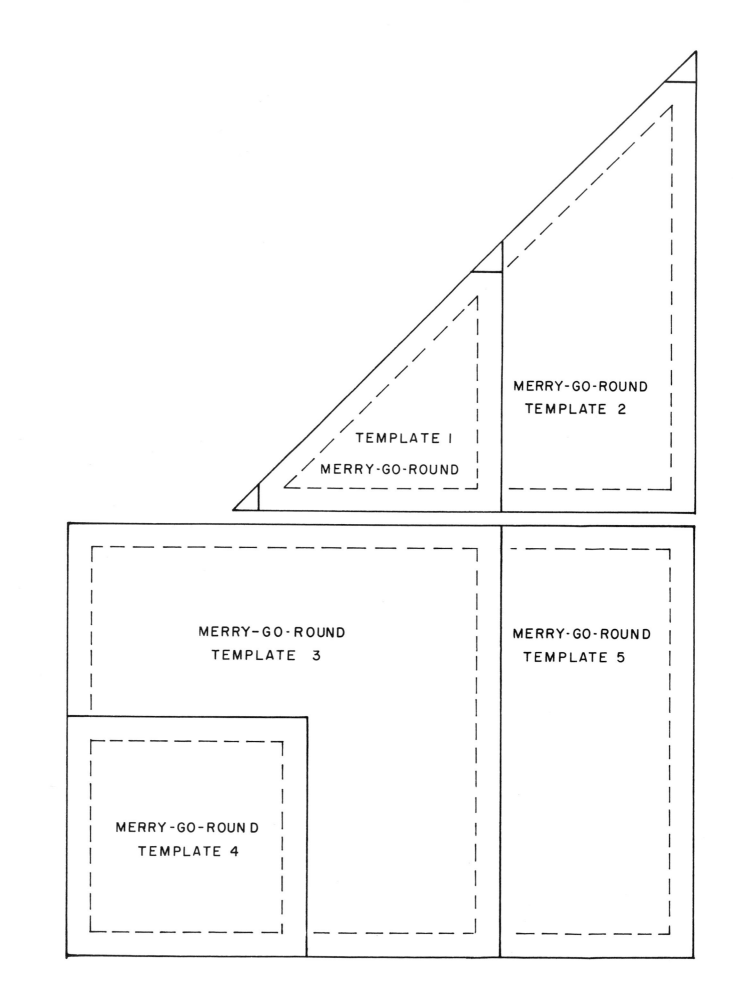

CLAY'S CHOICE

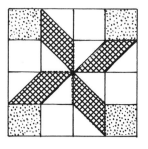

This traditional block is constructed as a four-patch from either squares and half-square triangles or, eliminating one seam, with squares, triangles and a parallelogram.

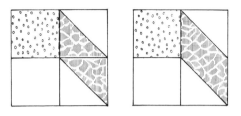

The four-patch is then rotated to produce a block with a pinwheel design.

The design for this baby's quilt or wallhanging began with a pattern of 8″ blocks. The twenty-four inner *Clay's Choice* blocks are pieced with a striped blue fabric for the pinwheel blades and a printed white fabric for the background. Superimposed over these twenty-four blocks are six blocks of a larger scale, 16″ on a side, spinning in the opposite direction.

The larger 16″ blocks are pieced with a slightly paler blue for the blades of the pinwheel. Where the small pinwheels overlap the larger pinwheels, a blue print is used. Transparency can be handled within a single color by careful selection of plain and patterned fabrics or by careful selection of two different patterns of similar colors.

In this overlapping of the two scales of *Clay's Choice*, the center of the larger pinwheel falls at the intersection of four of the smaller blocks, rather than on the center of one of the smaller pinwheels.

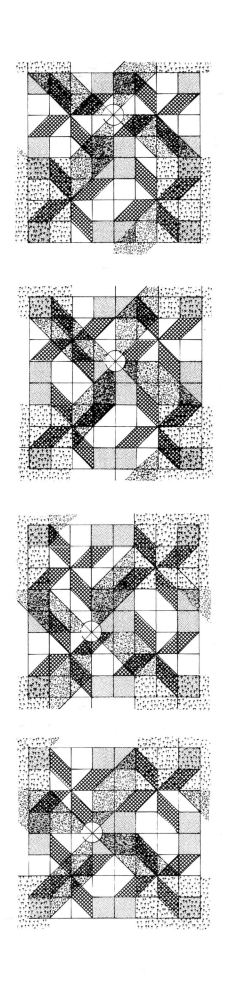

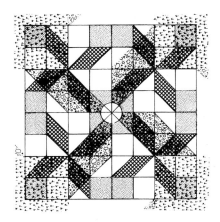

There are many different patterns possible, depending on where the center of the larger pinwheel is placed on the smaller block. Five variations are shown here. In each case, the center of the larger pinwheel is located on an intersection of the piecing in the smaller block.

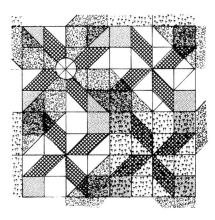

The center of the larger pattern could also be placed anywhere else on the smaller block, not on one of the piecing intersections. That will, however, significantly increase the number of templates required.

The central section of overlapped blocks can be constructed from one basic block, rotated around one corner. The basic block shown below, rotated around the indicated corner, produces the center pattern, as shown.

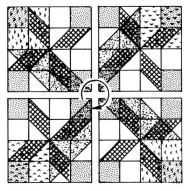

A ½″ lattice of a coral hand-dyed fabric separates the center blocks from additional 8″ blocks that make up the border. These border blocks are pieced with a large-print pastel fabric for the pinwheel blades and a Madras plaid for the background. Using such a large print in a pieced block serves to blur the edges of the pieces, especially when the dominant background colors of the print in the blades and the plaid in the background are the same as shown here.

The pattern of lines in the plaid in the border echoes the pattern of lines in the striped fabric used in the center and helps to tie the whole quilt together.

For my *Clay's Choice* quilt, as in much of my work, I created the pieces for the border blocks by stack-cutting the large-print pastel fabric for the pinwheel blades and playing with the resulting blocks, rather than carefully considering exactly what part of the design I wanted on each blade of each block. Besides being faster, stack-cutting such a print adds an element of chance which can yield some surprisingly good results. In the same way, accidental combinations of scraps on the floor may spark a design idea that you wouldn't have arrived at by patient toil. Try to keep your eyes open to what is happening around you. You are always the artist and can choose to pursue or discard each unforeseen event.

A line drawing of the center panel of the quilt with letters for the dark and medium colors can help in the construction process.

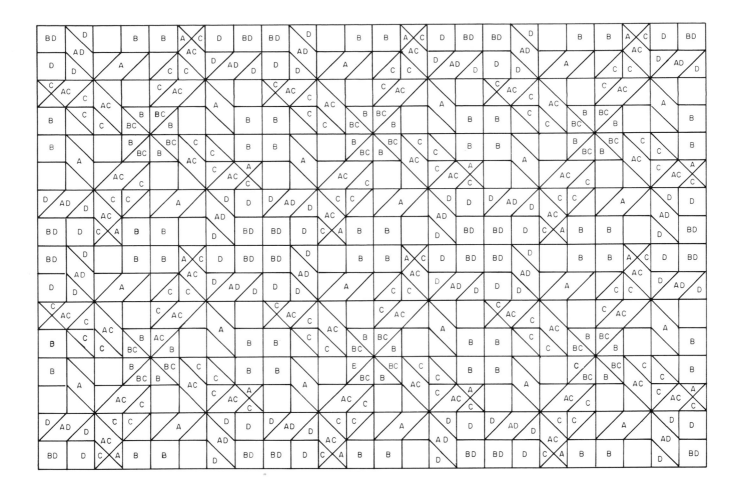

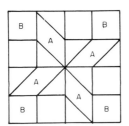

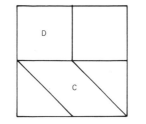

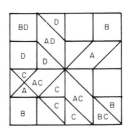

To make this 54½″ by 70½″ quilt, you will need:

COLOR	TEMPLATE					TOTAL YARDAGE
	1	**2**	**3**	**4**	**5**	
A	0	0	24	24	0	¼
B	48	24	0	0	0	½
C	0	72	24	0	0	½
D	24	48	0	0	0	⅜
AC	0	0	0	24	24	⅜
AD	0	0	0	24	0	¼
BC	0	24	0	0	0	¼
BD	24	0	0	0	0	¼
Background	48	96	24	0	0	1

For the borders:

A	0	0	0	96	0	½
B	96	0	0	0	0	½
Background	96	192	0	0	0	1
Lattice		Cut 2 (1″ by 48½″)				¼
		Cut 2 (1″ by 49½″)				
		Cut 4 (1″ by 8½″)				
Outer border		Cut 2 (3″ by 54½″)				¾
		Cut 2 (3″ by 65½″)				

Backing fabric: 3¼ yards of 45″ wide or 1⅞ yards of 60″ wide

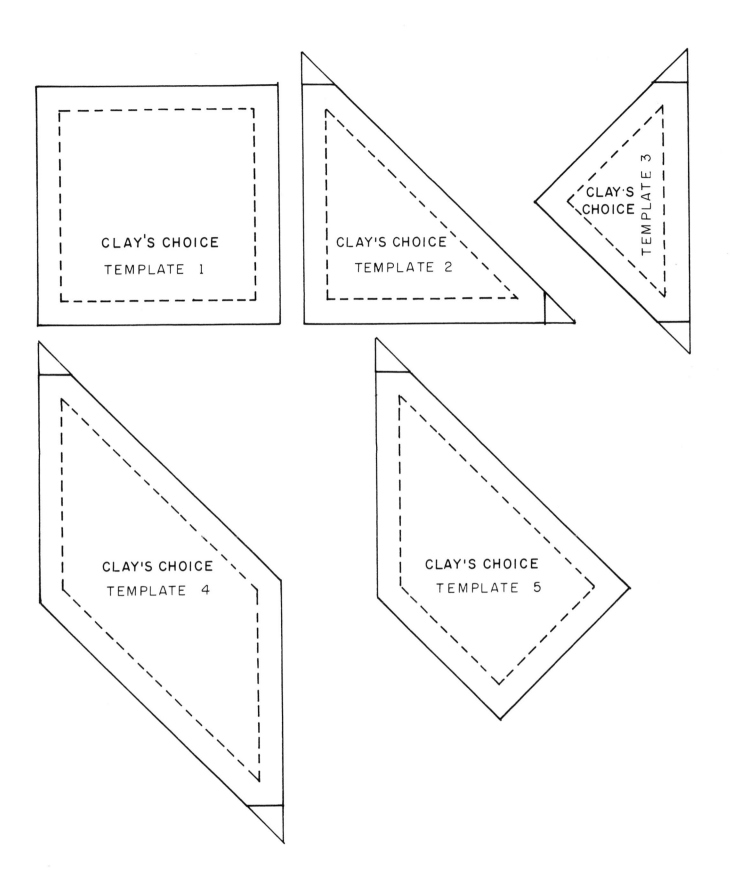

CLAY'S CHOICE
TEMPLATE 1

CLAY'S CHOICE
TEMPLATE 2

CLAY'S
CHOICE
TEMPLATE 3

CLAY'S CHOICE
TEMPLATE 4

CLAY'S CHOICE
TEMPLATE 5

CORN AND BEANS

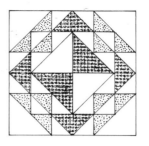

This traditional block stabilizes the dark hourglass shape in the center with symmetrical triangles in the corners. For this quilt, I decided to play with a yellow/green/blue transparency suggested by the colors of growing things, but with a background composed of an almost neutral gray/lavender rather than the traditional white. The design process began with a sketch of nine *Corn and Beans* blocks set in a square, but with the blocks in the upper right and lower left corners turned so that the dark hourglass shapes point toward the corners. The blocks are 24″ square. The colored triangles are light and dark blue.

Superimposed over this pattern of nine 24″ blocks is a larger *Corn and Beans* block with light and dark yellow triangles. Where parts of the yellow overlap the blue, I used light, medium or dark green.

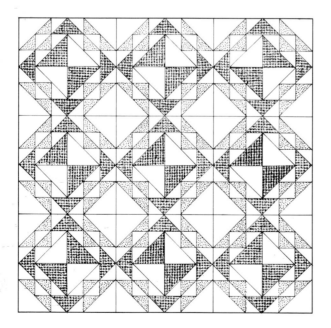

Further variation is present in that several different light yellows have been used, several different grayish lavenders in the background, etc., to produce a livelier surface.

The sunflower fabric that you see in this quilt was on my shelf. In terms of color, size and subject matter it seemed to belong in this *Corn and Beans* quilt. I used every bit of the half-yard I had, finally piecing together scraps to cut the last pieces. For the rectangular areas of sunflower fabric toward the center of the quilt, you will see that each rectangle is composed of three triangles. Although all three pieces are cut from the same sunflower print, in the big triangle the fabric is used wrong-side up. Visually, the rectangles read

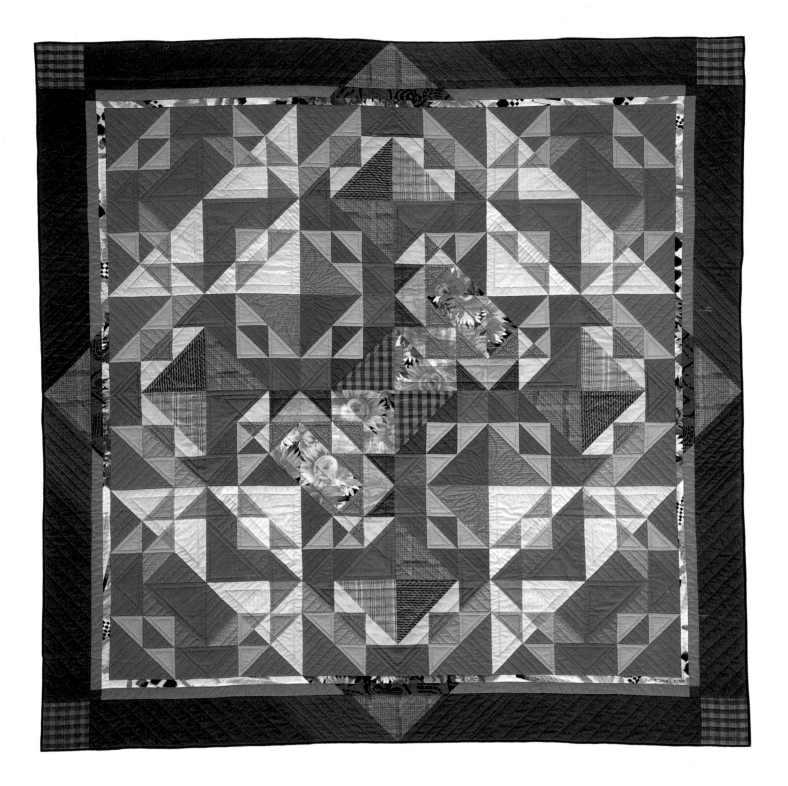

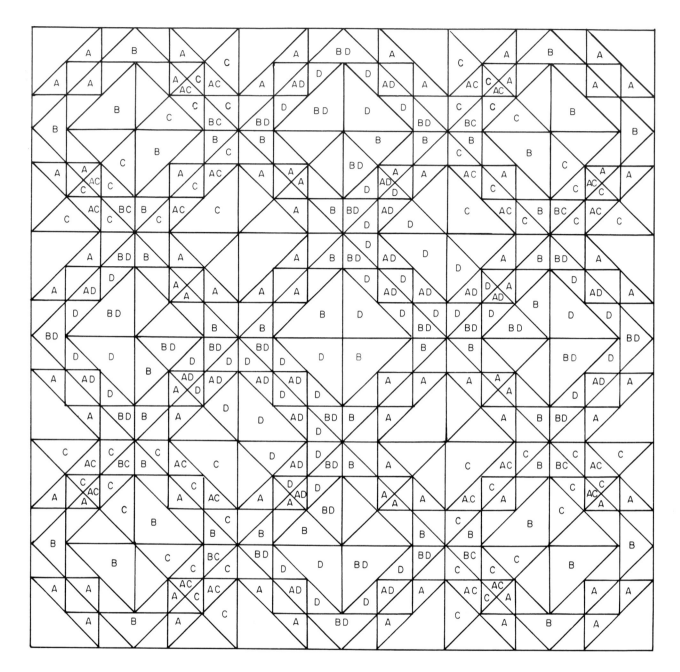

as sunflowers, but the subdued colors of the larger triangle subtly divide the area and keep it from becoming a hodgepodge of pattern.

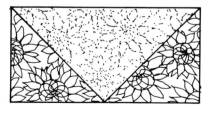

The borders of *Corn and Beans* are composed of two narrow bands of fabric containing the remaining snippets of the sunflower fabric, a solid peach fabric and another print. This second large print, of peach, green, black and white, echoes the little bits of black and white in the sunflower print and helps to give the quilt a little sparkle. The green plaid and cranberry red corner blocks are a necessary color addition to complement the body of the quilt.

I took a traditional approach to quilting this piece: by hand in the ditch, a grid of parallel lines radiating out from the center, and two areas of freely drawn quilted sunflowers. A needle-punched polyester batting was used.

To make an 89″ by 89″ quilt as illustrated, you will need:

COLOR	TEMPLATE				TOTAL YARDAGE
	1	**2**	**3**	**4**	
A light blue	0	0	58	20	¾
B dark blue	10	12	24	0	¾
C light yellow	4	16	28	8	¾
D dark yellow	8	4	34	4	¾
AC light green	0	0	16	8	¼
AD medium green	0	0	18	4	¼
BC medium blue/green	0	0	8	0	¼
BD dark green	4	8	16	0	½
Background	14	36	102	20	2

A series of three borders has been added to the 72½″ by 72½″ center:

Innermost border: Cut 2 (1½″ by 72½″)

Cut 2 (1½″ by 74½″)

In the quilt illustrated, this border has been pieced out of three fabrics.

If cut from one fabric: ½ yd.

Middle border: Cut 4 (2″ by 74½″)   ½ yd.

Cut 4 corner blocks (2″ by 2″)   scrap

Outer border: Cut 4 (6¼″ by 77½″)

In the quilt illustrated, this border has been pieced from three fabrics.

If cut from one fabric: 1½ yd.

Cut 4 corner blocks (6¼″ by 6¼″)   ¼ yd.

Backing fabric: 6½ yards of 45″ wide

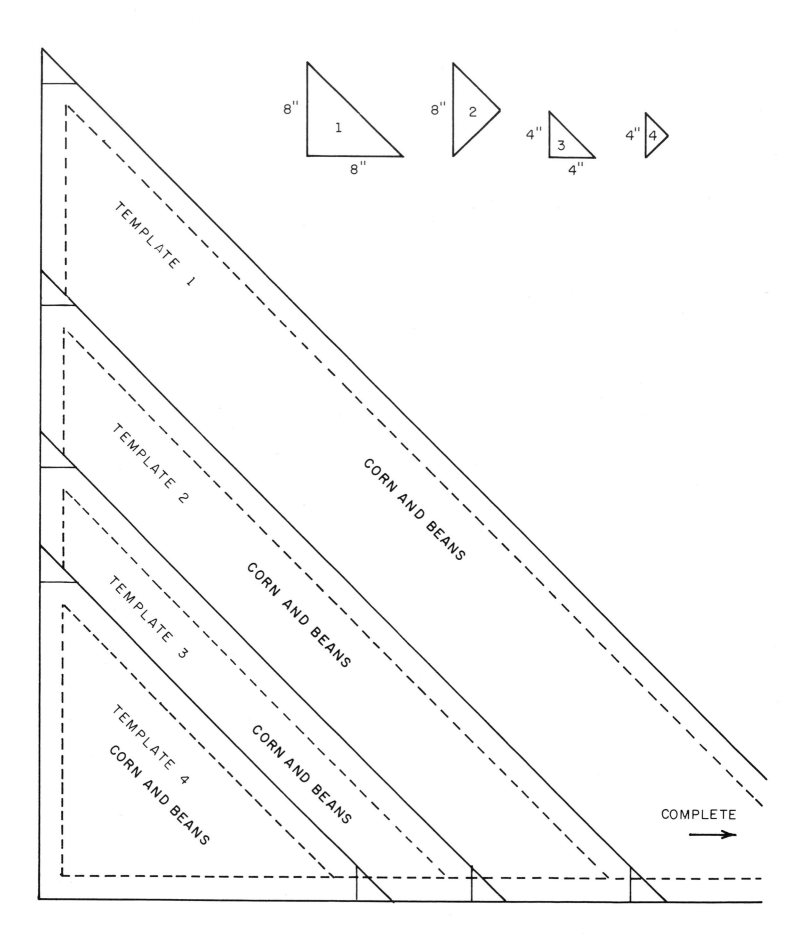

8" 1 8"

8" 2

4" 3 4"

4" 4

TEMPLATE 1

TEMPLATE 2

TEMPLATE 3

TEMPLATE 4

CORN AND BEANS

CORN AND BEANS

CORN AND BEANS

CORN AND BEANS

CORN AND BEANS

COMPLETE →

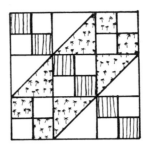

JACOB'S LADDER

The *Jacob's Ladder* block features a diagonal line of six squares crossed by four triangles on the opposite diagonal. It has long been a favorite among quiltmakers.

I arranged twenty-five 12″ blocks in a square. Each block faces in the same direction.

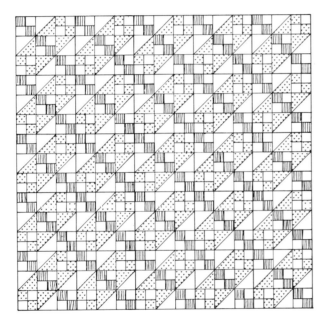

A second pattern was created with four 24″ blocks, in the same direction.

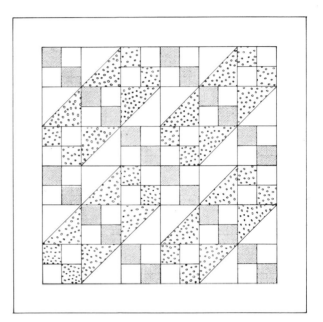

The second pattern does not overlap the first pattern completely, but leaves 6″ (half a block width) of the first pattern exposed as a border.

The regularity of the three major diagonals as originally drawn was a little boring. I made a slight change to the overlapped pattern, replacing some of the squares with larger triangles to add more variety to the diagonals.

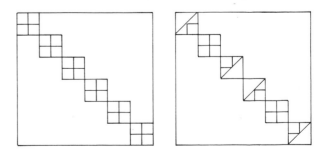

I decided to make a pair of *Jacob's Ladder* quilts from this diagram, differing rather wildly in the majority of the fabric choices, although the green and red diagonals are consistent.

Jacob's Ladder I began with an outer border of sixteen 12″ blocks cut from a white and yellow polka dot (Color A) on a light blue background fabric. The nine center 12″ blocks are cut from a white and lavender polka dot (Color A) on a medium blue background. The green diagonal squares (Color B) are from the same green ikat stripe in all twenty-five blocks.

Superimposed on this are the four 24″ blocks cut from yellow with a red-pink diagonal (Color B) made up of a red-pink solid and a red ikat stripe. While I have not attempted to make the transparency perfect in *Jacob's Ladder I*, being equally interested in working with the polka-dot fabrics and overall color combinations, the two scales of pattern are clearly visible.

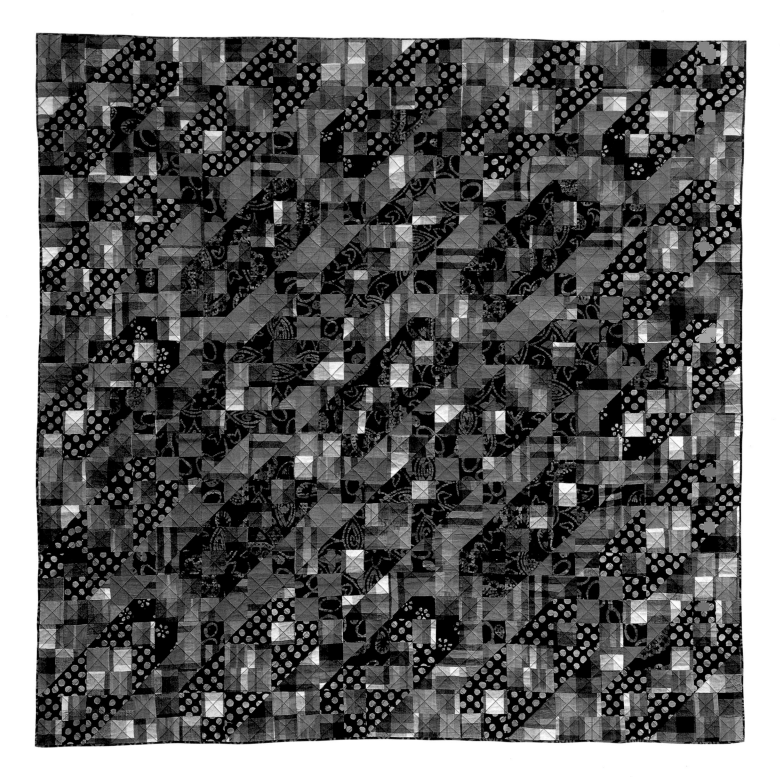

Jacob's Ladder II

Jacob's Ladder II is a much less obvious quilt. The 12″ blocks are pieced from three different indigo prints for Color A. (These fabrics are made with a resist pattern printed on top of woven plaids, which are then dyed dark blue. The underlying plaid makes a subtle echo of all the other plaids used in this quilt.) Color B, the diagonal squares, uses the same green ikat stripe as *Jacob's Ladder I*.

The pieces labeled C in *Jacob's Ladder II* are cut from a large orange/pink/green plaid with occasional lines of bright gold. For the pieces labeled AC, a fourth indigo print was used. A fifth indigo print is found in BD. Color D is very similar to the red used in the first quilt.

The background fabric was not a relatively uniform color this time, but a large plaid of black/white/red/blue/green, which was also used as the backing fabric. The pieces were stack-cut from the plaid without any consideration of what particular part of the plaid would show up in which piece. After all of the pieces for the quilt had been cut, they were pinned to the design wall and slight adjustments were made, switching pieces of the background plaid to scatter the lightest and darkest.

The use of a background fabric with this degree of color variation, this size of plaid and this much white/black contrast blurs the distinction between background and figure in the piecework. The pieced pattern is still there, but on a much more subtle level.

I worked with two very dissimilar machine quilting styles on these quilts. *Jacob's Ladder II* is quilted with a straight stitch, even-feed foot and black thread on a small diagonal grid. *Jacob's Ladder I* is free-motion machine quilted with a feed-dog cover plate and a darning foot in a continuous line zig zag pattern. Orange thread was used on the outer twelve inches of *Jacob's Ladder II*, blue thread in the center.

To make either 60½″ by 60½″ Jacob's Ladder as illustrated here, you will need:

FABRIC	TEMPLATE							YARDAGE
	1	**2**	**3**	**3R**	**4**	**5**	**5R**	
A	—	92	8	8	60	—	—	1⅝
B	—	86	—	—	—	—	—	⅝
C	—	32	—	—	16	16	16	¾
D	32	16	—	—	—	—	—	¼
AC	—	—	16	16	—	—	—	¼
BC	—	16	—	—	—	—	—	⅛
BD	—	32	—	—	16	—	—	⅜
Background	28	182	2	2	32	6	6	1⅝

Backing fabric: 3½ yards of 45″ wide

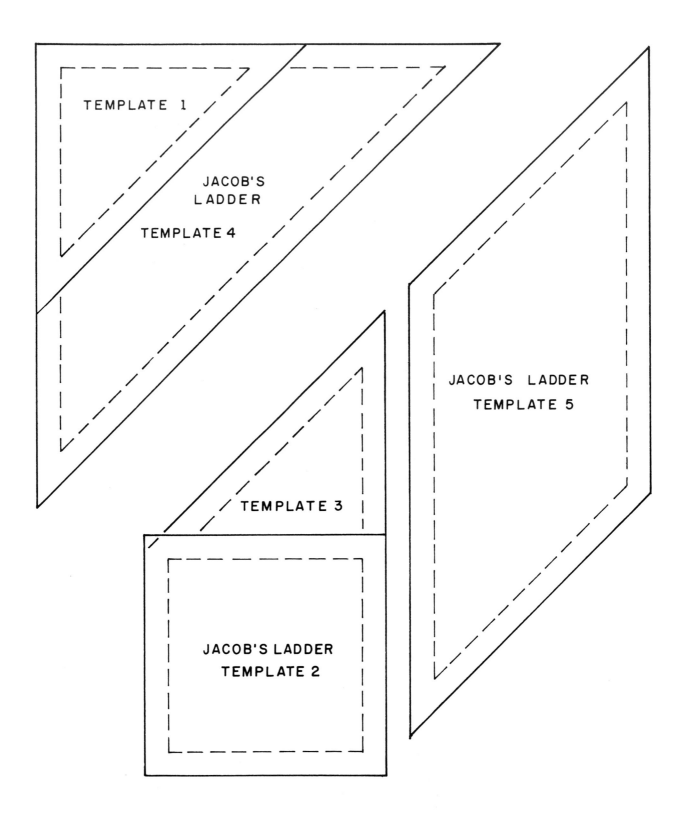

TEMPLATE 1

JACOB'S
LADDER

TEMPLATE 4

TEMPLATE 3

JACOB'S LADDER
TEMPLATE 5

JACOB'S LADDER
TEMPLATE 2

PICNIC IN THE CHERRY ORCHARD

The basket—in this case a picnic basket during cherry-picking season—is woven from rectangular pieces in a twill pattern.

Eight small baskets, each a 9″ block, are overlaid by the large picnic basket, a 27″ block.

The blocks are set on point, so that the baskets are upright, and bordered as a center medallion on a blue-and-white checked tablecloth.

The quilt was inspired by the wonderful printed cherry fabric. With two pie-cherry trees in my backyard, it was a familiar sight. Picking translucent scarlet cherries under a bright blue sky is a memorable experience. Clearly, any other large fruit or flower print fabric could inspire its own quilt.

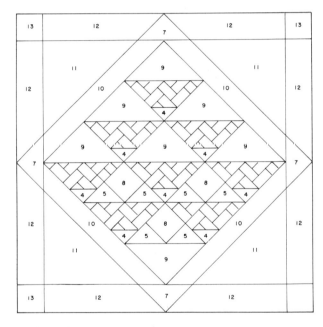

A few of the cherry clusters have been cut out of the fabric remnants and appliquéd to the pieced top. Prune away as much of the fabric covered by the appliqué as you can to make the appliqué blend into the surface of the quilt rather than sit on top of it like a patch.

The handle for the picnic basket is cut from a bias strip from one of the basket fabrics and hand appliquéd to the pieced top. Handles for the small baskets are quilted.

Picnic in the Cherry Orchard is hand quilted. It was first quilted in the ditch around the baskets and cherries. A band of feather quilting was sewn in the area cut from Template 10. The background is filled with freehand arcs, a very comfortable pattern to quilt by hand.

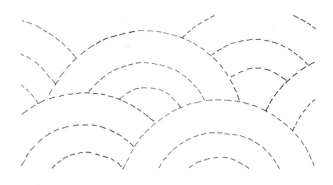

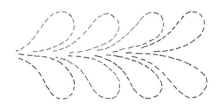

The quilt pictured here is 62″ square. I have scaled down the patterns and templates in this chapter to make a wallhanging of a more useable size. To make a 46½″ by 46½″ quilt, you will need:

FABRICS	TEMPLATES	CUT	YARDAGE
Cherries	4	3	¾
	9	7	
Baskets (assorted)	1	40	¾
	2	16	
	2R	8	
	3	32	
	4	5	
	5	6	
	6	8	
	8	3	
Purple triangle	7	4	¼
(corners of middle square)			

For the following very large templates, dimensions only are given. The dimensions listed are for the seam line. ASATAS = Add Seam Allowances To All Sides of all pieces to get the cutting line.

Inner border	10	4	½
Tablecloth	11	4	½
Outer border	12	4	1
	12R	4	
Corner blocks	13	4	¼

Backing fabric: 2¾ yards of 45″ wide or 1¾ yards of 60″ wide

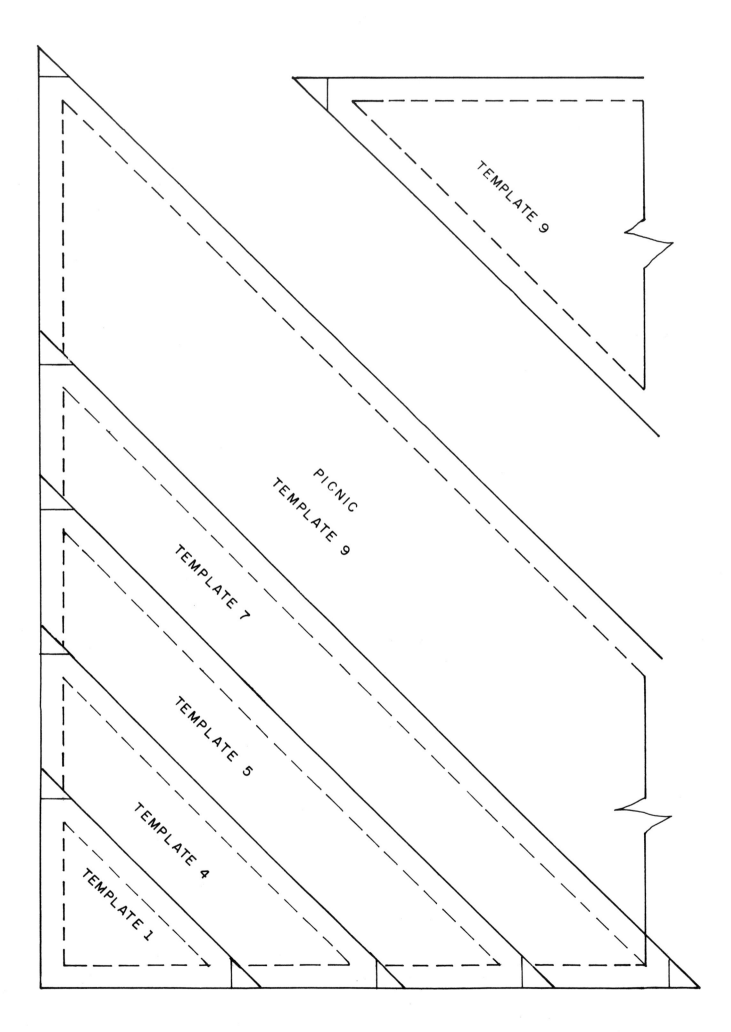

PICNIC
TEMPLATE 9

TEMPLATE 9

TEMPLATE 7

TEMPLATE 5

TEMPLATE 4

TEMPLATE 1

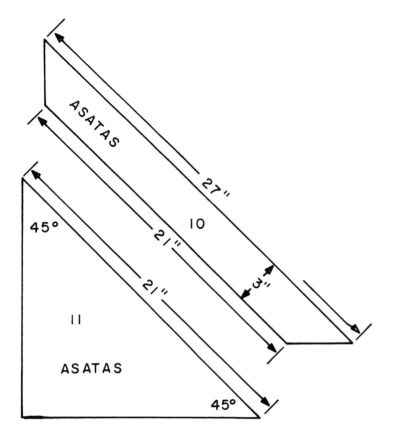

ASATAS

27"

10

21"

3"

21"

11

ASATAS

45°

45°

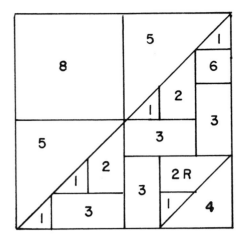

8   5   1

6

2

5   1   3

3

2   2R

1   3   3   1   4

ASATAS   ADD SEAM ALLOWANCE TO ALL SIDES

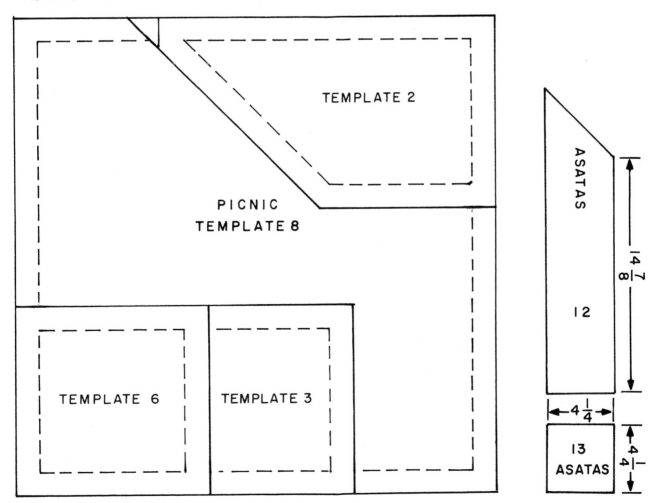

TEMPLATE 2

PICNIC
TEMPLATE 8

TEMPLATE 6   TEMPLATE 3

ASATAS

12

$14\frac{7}{8}$

$4\frac{1}{4}$

13
ASATAS

$4\frac{1}{4}$

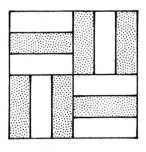

ROMAN SQUARE

The *Roman Square* block is built from a unit of three straight bars usually arranged in a basket weave pattern with lights and darks alternated.

Sometimes very simple blocks such as this one produce very interesting results when reverberant patterning is used. *Roman Square* begins with a 6″ grid of seven blocks by eight blocks, with an outer row that will form the border.

A larger diagonal grid of the same pattern is drawn to align with this first pattern.

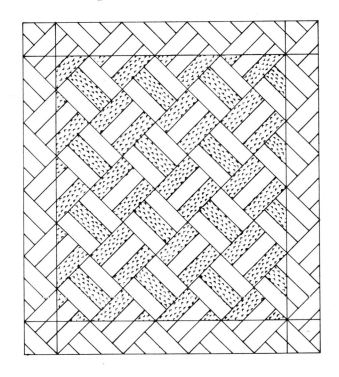

The overlapped patterns produce the design illustrated here. A careful examination will show that the center is composed of twenty-eight repetitions of two blocks, surrounded by a border.

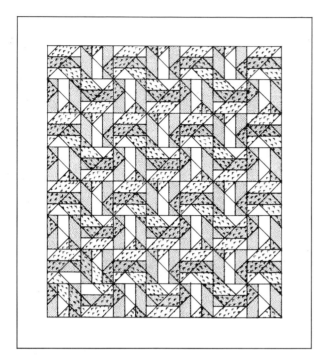

A precise following of the lines will lead to this piecing pattern.

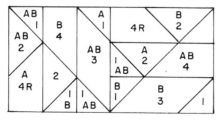

Piecing diagram 1

Combining adjacent pieces of the same color will produce this piecing pattern.

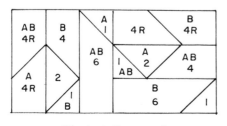

Piecing diagram 2

I prefer the first piecing pattern, which retains all of the seam lines of the original drawing. With many patterned fabrics, these extra seams will be visible as very subtle dislocations in the figuration.

The fabrics chosen for the center of my *Roman Square* quilt are two prints and two not-quite-solids.

Six-inch grid

Color A	Furnishing fabric shaded gray/gold/blue
Background	Wrong side of an off-white/black calico print, a not-quite-solid off-white

Diagonal grid

Color B	Black/off-white medium-size print, five-petalled flowers
Color AB	Gray/gold/lilac medium-size print, five-petalled flowers.

Transparency was handled differently in the border. At the top, the dark bars of the small-scale pattern were treated as though they were opaque and on top of the diagonal pattern. They are cut from a shaded peach fabric. At the bottom, the dark bars of the diagonal pattern are treated as though they were opaque and on top of the smaller blocks. They are cut from a black/off-white furnishing fabric print depicting a landscape with figures.

Quilting was done on the machine with off-white thread and an even-feed foot in a free-hand pattern of slightly curved lines.

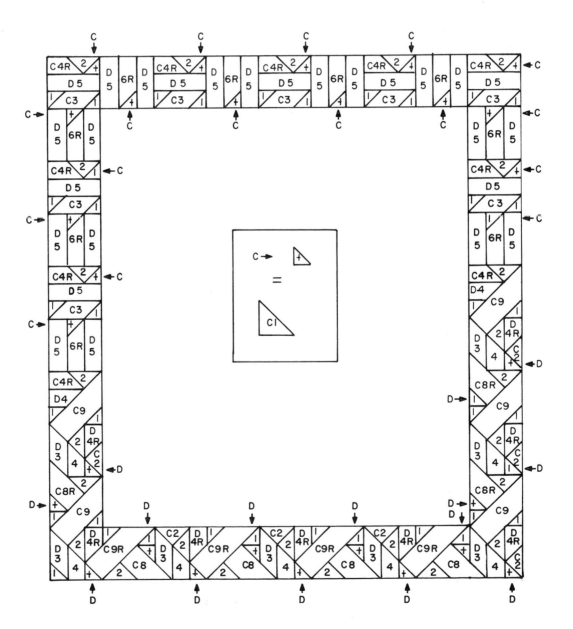

To make a 60″ by 54″ *Roman Square* quilt as illustrated here, you will need:

Piecing Diagram 1:   28 of each of two blocks

COLOR	TEMPLATE					YARDAGE
	1	**2**	**3**	**4**	**4R**	
A	28	28	—	—	28	⅝
B	56	28	28	28	—	1
AB	84	28	28	28	—	1
Background	56	28	—	—	28	⅝

Piecing Diagram 2:   28 of each of two blocks

COLOR	TEMPLATE					YARDAGE
	1	**2**	**4**	**4R**	**6**	
A	28	28	—	28	—	⅝
B	28	—	28	28	28	1
AB	28	—	28	28	28	1
Background	28	28	—	28	—	⅝

Border:

COLOR	TEMPLATE											YARDAGE
	1	**2**	**3**	**4**	**4R**	**5**	**6R**	**8**	**8R**	**9**	**9R**	
C	17	7	8	—	10	—	—	4	3	5	4	1
D	15	—	8	2	8	26	—	—	—	—	—	¾
Bkgd.	32	25	—	8	—	—	9	—	—	—	—	¾

Backing fabric: 3¼ yards of 45″ wide or 1⅞ yards of 60″ wide

Roman Square Pinwheels

If you go back to the line drawing on page 104 and ignore the coloring scheme, you can pick out a pattern of pinwheels.

The pinwheel quilt is constructed of forty-eight repetitions of this block:

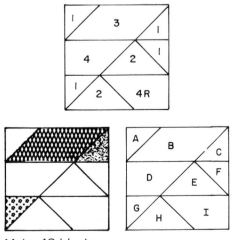

Make 48 blocks

For my *Roman Square Pinwheels* quilt, I picked nine fabrics, made forty-eight blocks, and arranged them according to the line drawing at the left.

The body of the quilt is tied to the border by completing the small pink pinwheels at the top and bottom and the small blue and white dotted pinwheels at the sides in the narrow inner border. Corner blocks and a white/multi-colored stripe complete the frame for the quilt.

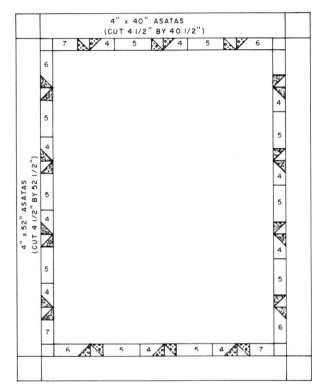

Quilting was done on the machine using a darning foot and feed-dog cover plate with blue thread in an all-over freehand pattern.

To make a 60½″ by 48½″ quilt as illustrated here, you will need:

COLOR	TEMPLATE								YARDAGE
	1	2	3	4	4R	5	6	7	
A (orange print)	48	—	—	—	—	—	—	—	¼
B (large dark print)	—	—	48	—	—	—	—	—	⅜
C (blue/white polka dot)	64	—	—	—	—	—	—	—	⅜
D (multi-color polka dot)	—	—	—	48	—	—	—	—	⅜
E (blue)	—	48	—	—	—	—	—	—	⅜
F (green)	48	—	—	—	—	—	—	—	¼
G (pink)	60	—	—	—	—	—	—	—	⅜
H (blue/green shaded)	—	48	—	—	—	—	—	—	⅜
I (blue/green with pink dots)	—	—	—	—	48	—	—	—	⅜
Inner border	14	—	—	10	—	10	4	4	½

Inner border:	Cut 4 corner blocks (2½″ by 2½″) from scrap	
Outer borders:	Cut 2 (4½″ by 52½″)	1½
	Cut 2 (4½″ by 40½″)	
	Cut 4 corner blocks (4½″ by 4½″) from scrap	

Backing fabric: 3 yards of 45″ wide or 1⅞ yards of 60″ wide

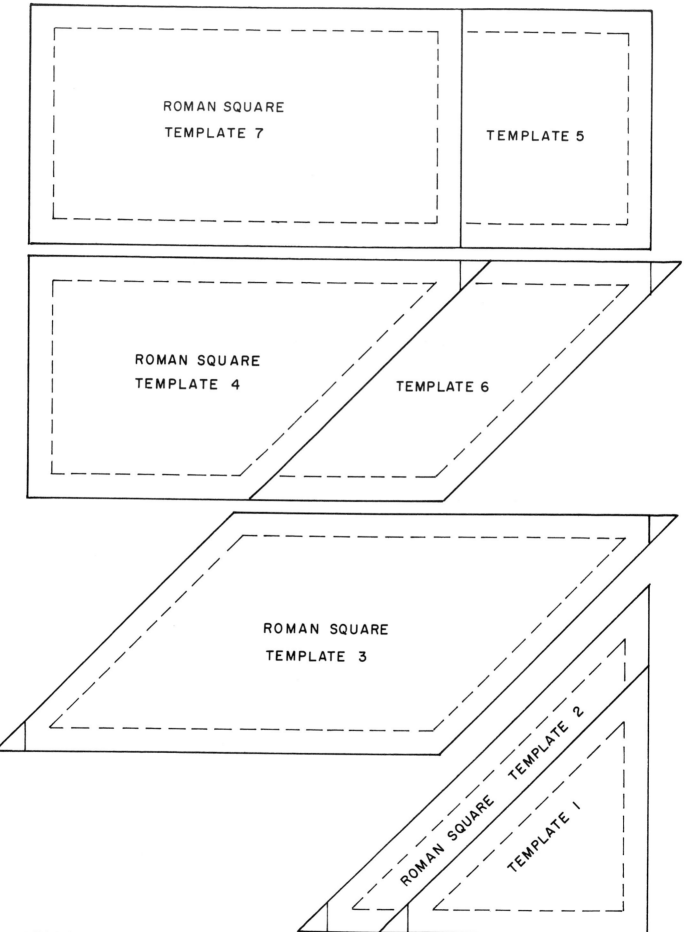

ROMAN SQUARE
TEMPLATE 7

TEMPLATE 5

ROMAN SQUARE
TEMPLATE 4

TEMPLATE 6

ROMAN SQUARE
TEMPLATE 3

ROMAN SQUARE   TEMPLATE 2

TEMPLATE I

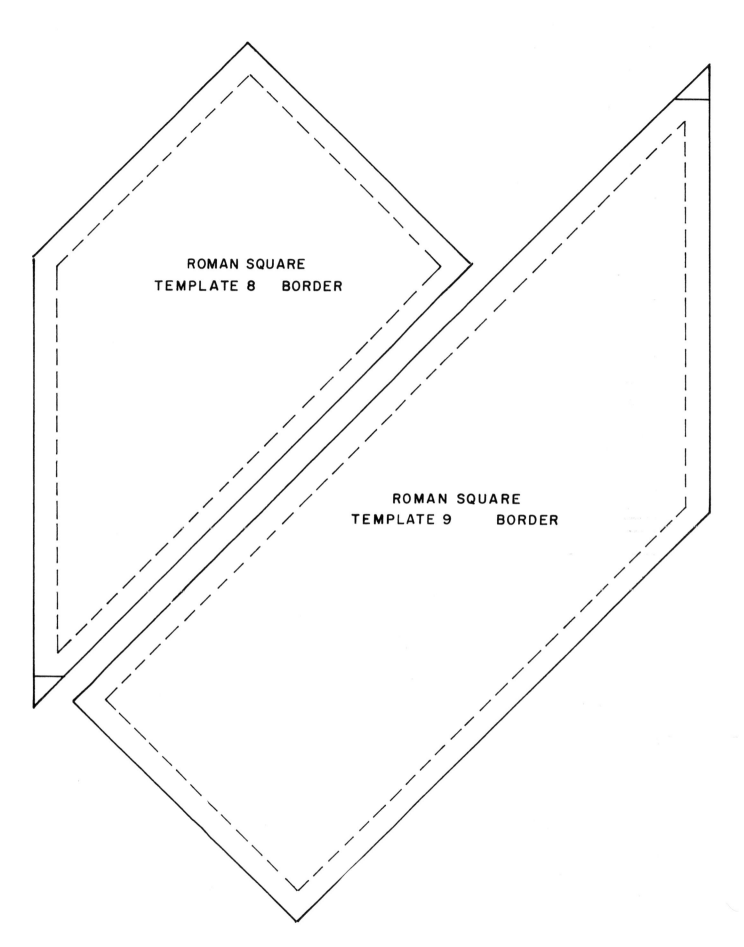

ROMAN SQUARE
TEMPLATE 8   BORDER

ROMAN SQUARE
TEMPLATE 9   BORDER

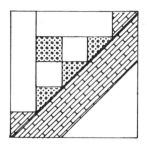

KING'S CROWN

King's Crown is another traditional block based on a nine-patch and pieced from squares, small triangles, a larger triangle and strips. For this quilt I made a grid of 15″ *King's Crown* blocks set straight.

Larger blocks are set on point. The scale of the larger blocks was chosen so that the side is the length of the diagonal of the 15″ block (21.21″).

113   KING'S CROWN

Overlapping the two scales of pattern produces the design shown here.

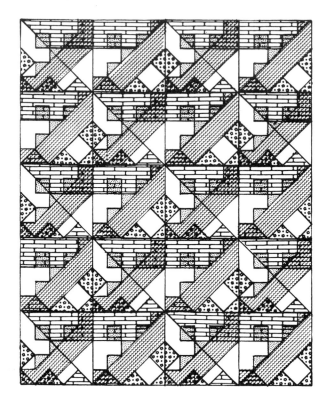

Fabrics chosen were mainly black and white, with a few small pieces of purple, red, periwinkle and topaz. The unusual peacock fabric in indigo, purple and green/gold is from Italy, manufactured with a wax-resist indigo dye.

In *King's Crown*, two co-ordinated drapery fabrics were used, one with a black background and ginko leaves in shaded blues and purples, and the other of black with narrow bars of color at different angles.

The border of *King's Crown* was designed after the body of the quilt was pieced. It was chosen to emphasize the diagonal bars in the block. An asymmetric arrangement of diagonal stripes, with more black at the bottom and more white at the top, it makes a relatively simple block quilt into something much more exciting.

The quilting pattern for *King's Crown* is traditional in that it echoes the piecing pattern, but it was done on the sewing machine with black and metallic threads. Metallic threads are now available that work quite well in the machine and can add a little sparkle in strategic spots.

To make a quilt like the *King's Crown* illustrated, refer to the color map for the two blocks.

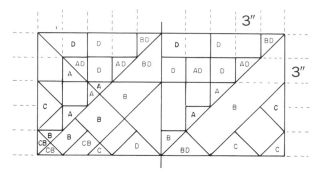

Ten of each of the two pattern blocks shown at the top above will produce a pieced center 60½″ high by 75½″ long. The asymmetric border is 8″ wide, making the finished size 76½″ wide by 91½″ long.

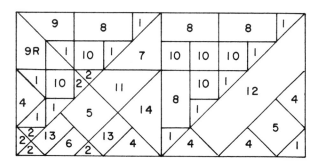

To make a 91½″ by 76½″ quilt as illustrated here, you will need:

TEMPLATE	COLOR							
	A	B	C	D	AD	CB	BD	Background
1	40	10	10	—	30	—	20	20
2	20	10	10	—	—	20	—	—
4	—	—	30	10	—	—	10	—
5	—	10	—	—	—	—	—	10
6	—	—	—	—	—	10	—	—
7	—	—	—	—	—	—	10	—
8	—	—	—	30	—	—	—	10
9	—	—	—	10	—	—	—	—
9R	—	—	—	—	—	—	—	10
10	—	—	—	30	10	—	—	20
11	—	10	—	—	—	—	—	—
12	—	10	—	—	—	—	—	—
13	—	10	—	—	—	—	—	10
14	—	—	—	—	—	—	—	10
Yardage	⅜	1½	½	¾	⅜	¼	½	1½

Borders: I will leave the exact border composition to you. The center section should measure 60½″ by 75½″. You will need almost 8 yards of a strip-pieced border, 8½″ wide, or about 2 yards of fabric.

Backing fabric: 5¼ yards of 45″ wide or 4½ yards of 60″ wide.

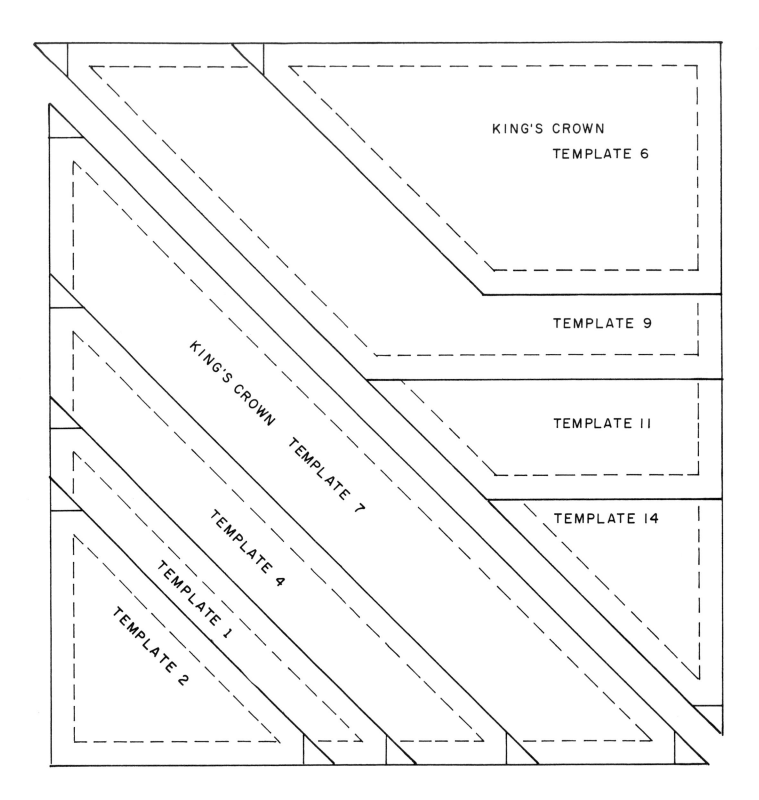

KING'S CROWN

TEMPLATE 6

TEMPLATE 9

TEMPLATE 11

TEMPLATE 14

KING'S CROWN TEMPLATE 7

TEMPLATE 4

TEMPLATE 1

TEMPLATE 2

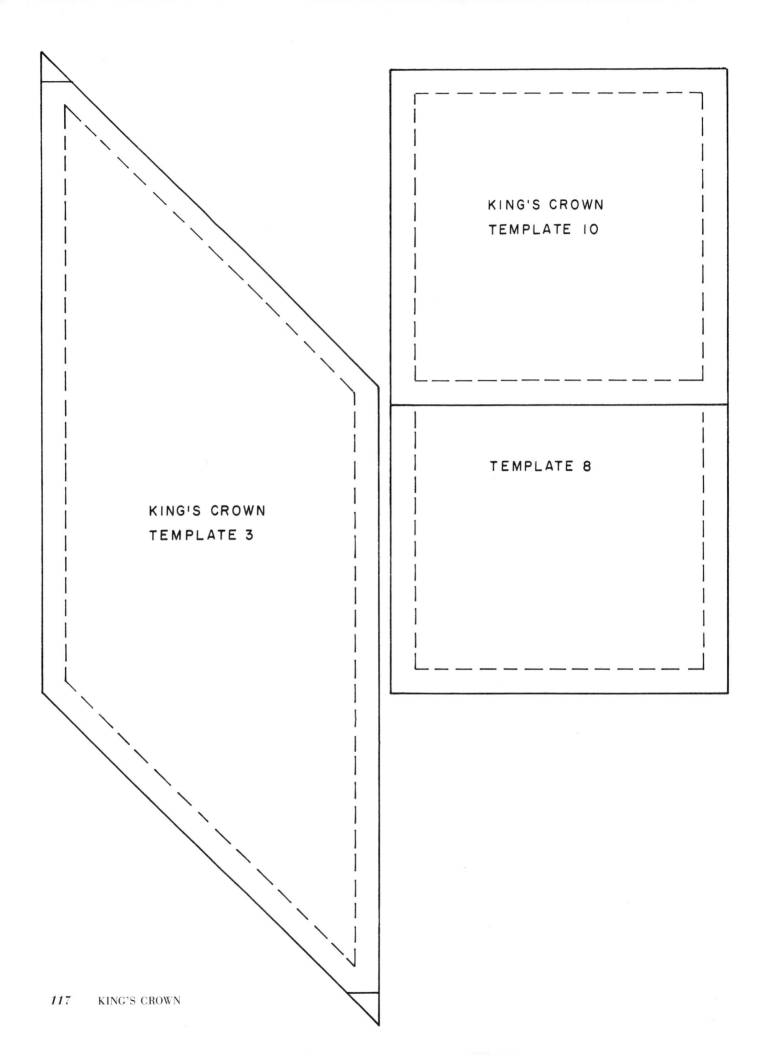

KING'S CROWN
TEMPLATE 10

TEMPLATE 8

KING'S CROWN
TEMPLATE 3

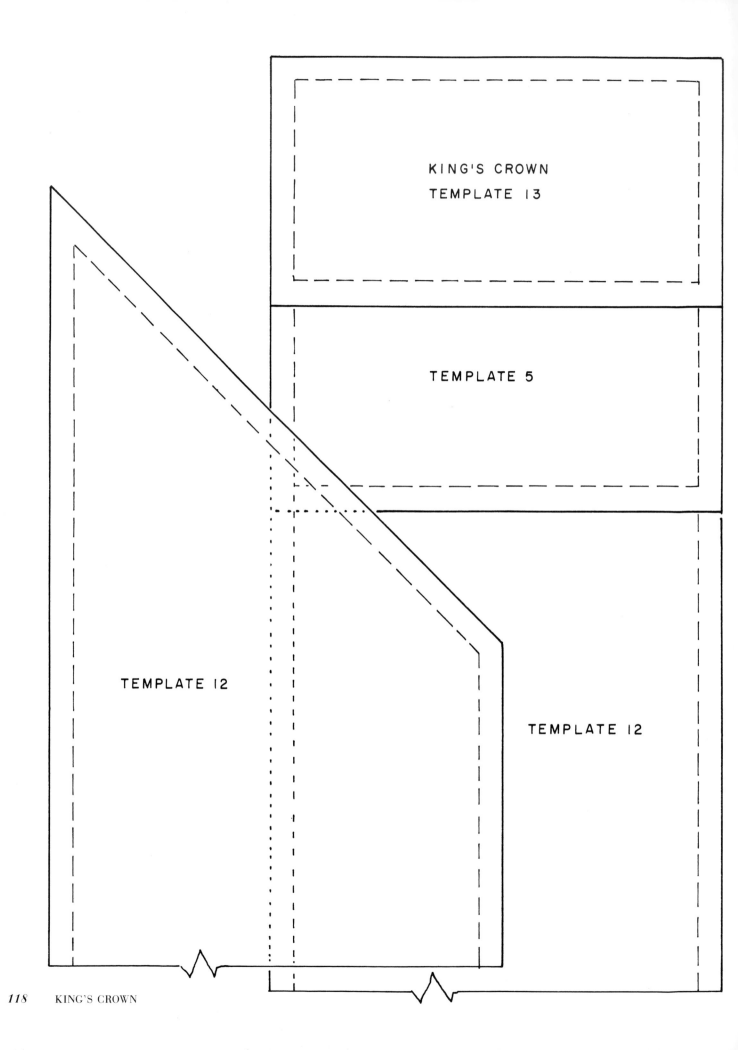

KING'S CROWN
TEMPLATE 13

TEMPLATE 5

TEMPLATE 12

TEMPLATE 12

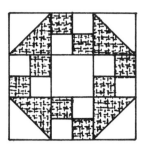

PRAIRIE QUEEN

An infrequently-used traditional block, *Prairie Queen* is developed from a nine-patch. It is composed of a central square with four small four-patches and four diagonally divided corner blocks around it.

This *Prairie Queen* quilt is designed in three sections, using two scales of pattern. It is treated as an exercise in transparency and opacity. The smaller block is a 9″ square.

The same pattern is then drawn with an 18″ block.

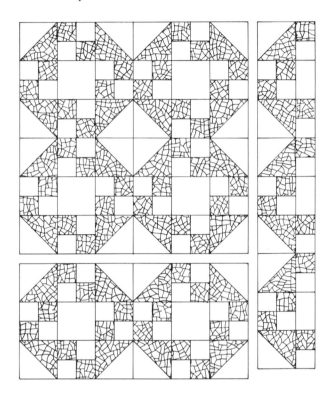

A black mottled furnishing fabric is used for the background, rather than the traditional white.

At the upper left are sixteen 9″ blocks overlapped by four transparent 18″ blocks. At the lower left, the two 18″ blocks are treated as though they were opaque and on top of the eight 9″ blocks. At the right, six 9″ blocks are opaque and on top of three half-blocks of the 18″ pattern.

Thus, in the upper-left panel, the two patterns are transparent; where they overlap, Color AB is used. At the lower left, the 18″ pattern is complete and uninterrupted; the 9″ pattern peeks out around the edges. At the right, the 9″ pattern is complete, with the 18″ pattern showing in the spaces. A solid lavender fabric used in the central squares of the blocks in the right column produces a nice repetition along the edge.

The sub-assembly units will speed up the construction of the blocks. See page 19 for some quick-piecing methods.

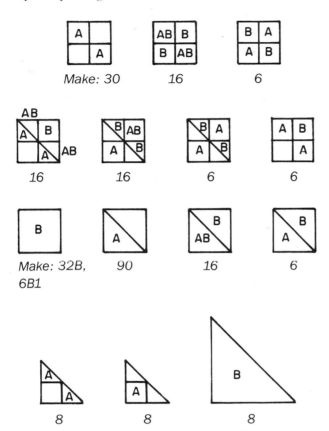

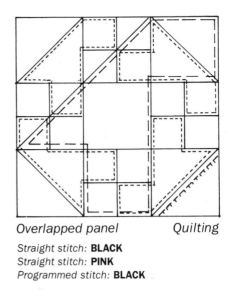

Overlapped panel　　　　*Quilting*

Straight stitch: **BLACK**
Straight stitch: **PINK**
Programmed stitch: **BLACK**

The lower-left panel is made of eight blocks, rotated around the corner with the + sign in it.

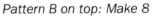

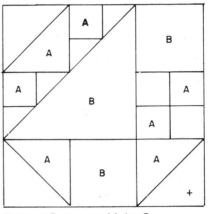

Pattern B on top: Make 8

The upper-left panel is made of sixteen of the blocks illustrated here, rotated around the corner indicated by a star.

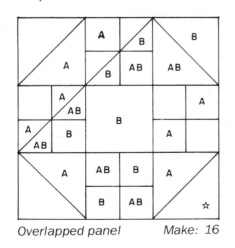

Overlapped panel　　　　*Make: 16*

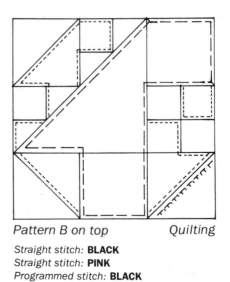

Pattern B on top　　　　*Quilting*

Straight stitch: **BLACK**
Straight stitch: **PINK**
Programmed stitch: **BLACK**

Six of the blocks make up the right panel.

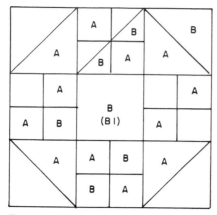

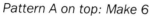

Pattern A on top: Make 6

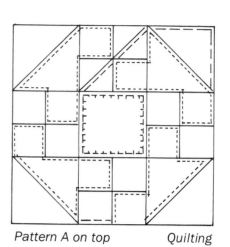

Pattern A on top   *Quilting*

Straight stitch: **BLACK**
Straight stitch: **PINK**
Programmed stitch: **LAVENDER**

Overlapped panel

Pattern B on top

Pattern A on top

The center square in each of these six blocks was cut from a solid lavender fabric (Color B1).

The border is handled is a less traditional manner than in most of the other quilts in the book. The dimensions of the strips and squares in the border relate to the areas of the pieces in the quilt, but the border fabrics are quite different, Dutch-wax indigo prints and ikat stripes for the most part.

Quilting was done on the machine using pink, lavender or black thread and a straight stitch with an even-feed foot, ¼" inside the seam lines of the blocks. In the indicated places in the blocks and in the borders, a programmed stitch was used.

To make a 63" by 52" quilt as illustrated here, you will need:

COLOR	TEMPLATE					YARDAGE
	1	2	3	4	5	
A blue	32	128	96	—	—	1⅛
B pink	44	66	22	32	8	1¼
AB purple	32	48	16	—	—	½
B1 lavender	—	—	—	6	—	¼
Background black	76	82	90	—	—	1⅛

Top inner border:
Cut 1 (3½" by 36½") Indigo print
Cut 2 (Template 4) Pink ikat
Cut 1 (Template 4) Purple ikat

Bottom inner border:
Cut 1 (2" by 36½") Indigo print
Cut 1 (2" by 9½") Pink ikat
Cut 1 (3½" by 39½") Pink ikat
Cut 2 (Template 4) Indigo print
Cut 1 (Template 4) Purple ikat

Left inner border:
Cut 1 (3½" by 11") Indigo print
Cut 1 (3½" by 9½") Pink ikat
Cut 1 (3½" by 39½") Indigo print

Background fabric: 3⅛ yards of 45" wide or 1⅞ yards of 60" wide

Right inner border:
Cut 1 (3½" by 14") Indigo print
Cut 1 (3½" by 9½") Pink ikat
Cut 1 (3½" by 39½") Indigo print

Outer edge:
Cut 2 (1½" by 41½") Red ikat
Cut 2 (1½" by 64") Red ikat

Border Yardage:	3 indigo prints	¼ yd. of each
	Pink ikat	¼
	Red ikat	¼
	Purple ikat	scrap

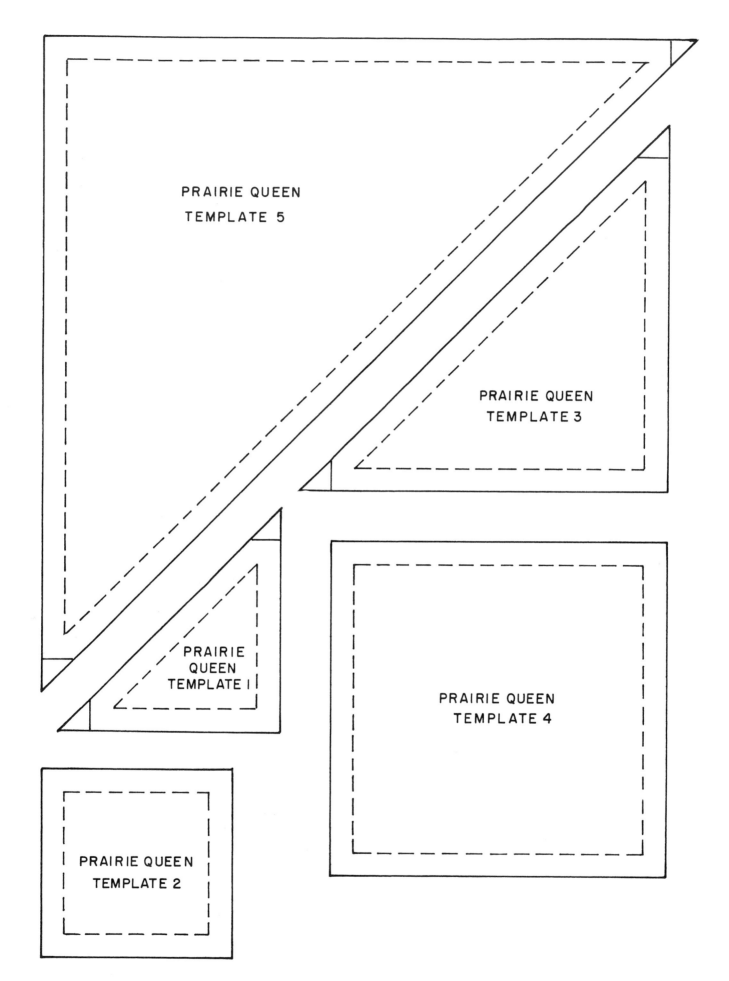

PRAIRIE QUEEN
TEMPLATE 5

PRAIRIE QUEEN
TEMPLATE 3

PRAIRIE
QUEEN
TEMPLATE 1

PRAIRIE QUEEN
TEMPLATE 4

PRAIRIE QUEEN
TEMPLATE 2

SNOWFLAKE

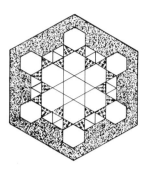

Crystal structures fascinate me. Because of the structure of the molecule of water, water crystals such as snowflakes form patterns of hexagons and equilateral triangles.

Piecing a quilt from a grid of equilateral triangles is no more difficult than piecing one of squares and right triangles. A convenient way to work out a design is on equilateral triangle graph paper. This specialty graph paper is available at some quilt shops, some mail-order quilting suppliers, and even some stationery stores. It is composed of a grid of equilateral triangles rather than the familiar grid of squares.

Traditional patterns such as *Grandmother's Flower Garden* and *Thousand Pyramids* can be drawn on this paper, as well as original designs.

This snowflake pattern is symmetrical and composed of hexagons and equilateral triangles. Six *Snowflake* blocks are arranged in a ring around a central block. After some experimenta-

tion, I decided to leave some space (sashing) between the snowflakes, rather than drawing them with the points touching.

A second pattern was drawn of a single larger version of the same *Snowflake* block radiating from the center of the quilt.

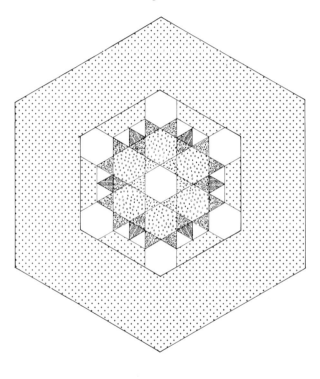

Overlapping the two patterns produces a design of great complexity.

I eliminated some of the seam lines (for instance, most of the line that forms the hexagon circumscribing each snowflake) in order to simplify construction and to reduce the number of templates required. On the next page is the final piecing pattern.

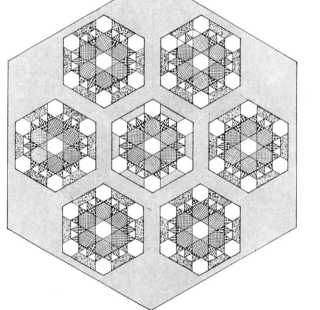

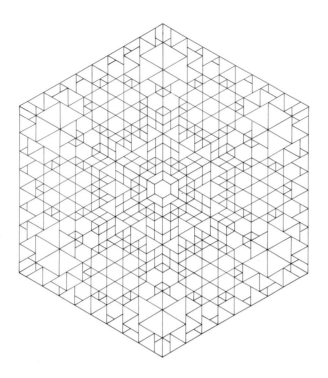

The design of this quilt breaks down into six identical wedges surrounding a small central hexagon.

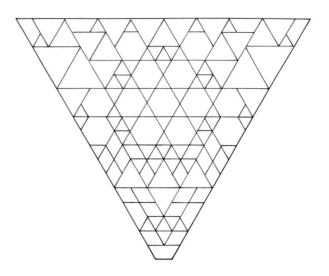

The quilt was finished as a hexagon, the outer edges of the design being filled with triangles and trapezoids of various shades of gray.

Another solution to finishing hexagonal designs is to fill out the corners to make the quilt rectangular. Here, for example, the corners have been filled with various arrangements of triangles.

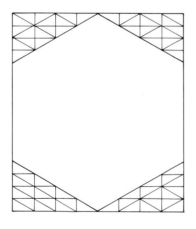

Highlights and shadows on snow can be a myriad of subtle colors in addition to the conventional white. Blues, greens, lavenders, roses and golds are used here. Interesting results would be achieved if you were to use exclusively "white" fabrics, but with different light-reflecting properties—silks, satins, brocades, polished cottons, grosgrains, lamés, metallics and iridescent fabrics.

After working out the color placement for one of these wedges on the design wall, I cut and sewed all six.

The lacy patterns of snowflakes can be enhanced by machine quilting with some of the fancy stitch capabilities of some new sewing machines. Machine quilting a piece of this size is much easier if the work is done in sections like the wedges here. The wedges are much less bulky under the arm of the machine.

In this process, first complete all of the quilting in the shaded area on each wedge. Then begin to assemble the quilt by quilt-as-you-go method 2 (see page 25).

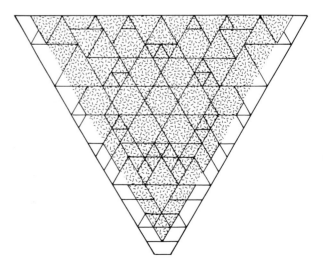

Trim the batting to the size of the top, and the backing fabric ¼″ larger. Then sew the wedges together in pairs, machine piecing the edges of the tops carefully to match the designs, and keeping the batting and backing free.

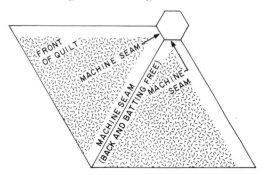

Turning the pairs backside up, smooth the edges of the batting together and overlap the backings, turning under the top edge and hemming it down by hand.

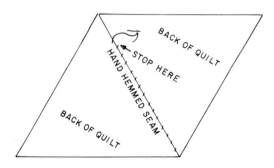

With the seam on the back finished, turn the pairs right side up and complete the quilting over the finished seam to within 2″ of the center edge.

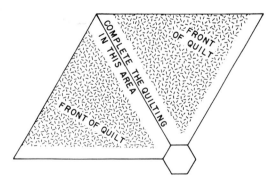

There is one small solid hexagon pieced into the very center of this quilt. This was machine pieced to one of the pairs of wedges during the quilt-as-you-go assembly process. It makes a very neat center to the quilt, although it does complicate the assembly process. (A simpler approach, but bulky, would divide this central hexagon into six equilateral triangles and add one of these to each of the wedges. The assembly seams on both the top and back would then meet in the center of the quilt.)

Join two of the quilted pairs of wedges together in a similar way and sew them to the central hexagon.

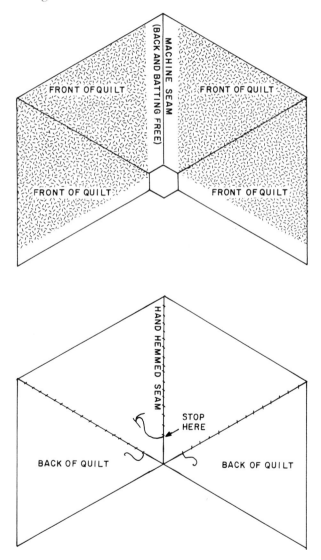

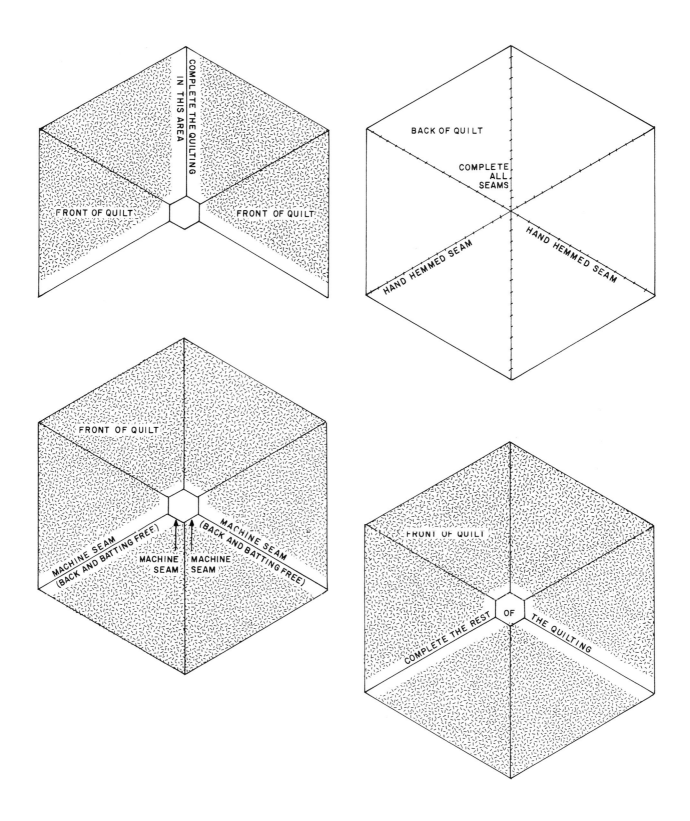

The quilting designs for the *Snowflake* quilt were chosen to explore some of the fancy stitches programmed into my machine and to experiment with inventing fancy stitches on its programming attachment. The outer gray edge was quilted/tied with a scattering of single machine-stitched snowflakes sewn with silver metallic thread. The machine can be set to tie off such a pattern at its start and finish. The smaller pieced snowflake patterns were quilted with white size 50 cotton thread in the four different fancy stitches shown below the stitched snowflakes. I designed and pro-

grammed into the machine the bottom row of stitching shown here and used it to quilt the main ribs of each snowflake.

For the larger *Snowflake* pattern, the quilting was done with the same stitch patterns, but at an expanded scale. A variegated blue-violet-pink-yellow-green size 70 tatting and crochet cotton thread was used in the top spool. I enjoy using variegated threads for machine quilting, but they are sometimes hard to find. The tatting cotton comes in good variegated colors and works well in my machine.

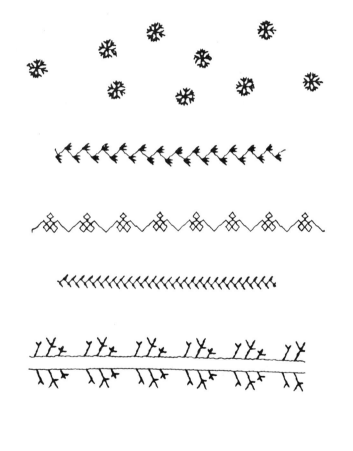

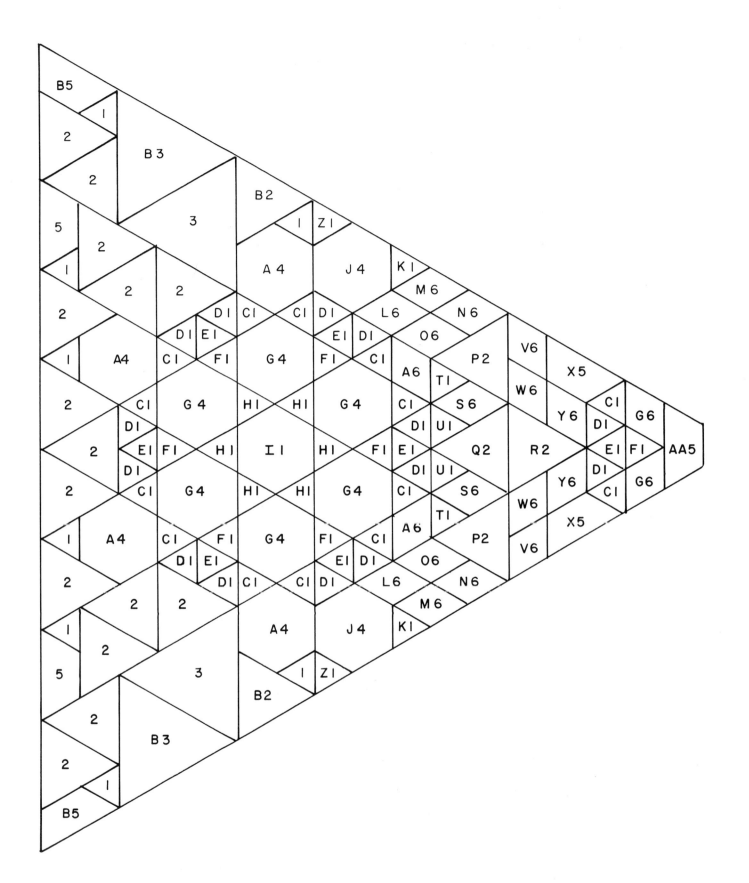

Using the templates here will produce a quilt about 90″ by 80″. You will need:

COLOR	TEMPLATE								YARDAGE
	1	2	3	4	5	5R	6	6R	
A White	—	—	—	24	—	—	6	6	⅝
B Light gray	—	12	12	—	6	6	—	—	⅞
C Purple	84	—	—	—	—	—	—	—	¾
D Light blue	84	—	—	—	—	—	—	—	¾
E Light green	42	—	—	—	—	—	—	—	½
F Purple	42	—	—	—	—	—	—	—	½
G Shaded blue	—	—	—	36	—	—	6	6	⅞
H Blue/pink	36	—	—	—	—	—	—	—	⅜
I Sky blue	—	—	—	6	—	—	—	—	¼
J Peach	—	—	—	12	—	—	—	—	⅜
K Yellow	12	—	—	—	—	—	—	—	⅛
L Light orange	—	—	—	—	—	—	6	6	⅛
M Yellow	—	—	—	—	—	—	6	6	⅛
N Coral	—	—	—	—	—	—	6	6	⅛
O Light yellow	—	—	—	—	—	—	6	6	⅛
P Purple	—	12	—	—	—	—	—	—	⅛
Q Pink/green	—	6	—	—	—	—	—	—	⅛
R Blue	—	6	—	—	—	—	—	—	⅛
S Blue print	—	—	—	—	—	—	6	6	⅛
T Purple	12	—	—	—	—	—	—	—	⅛
U Pale blue	12	—	—	—	—	—	—	—	⅛
V Pink/lavender	—	—	—	—	—	—	6	6	⅛
W Pale yellow	—	—	—	—	—	—	6	6	⅛
X Lavender	—	—	—	—	6	6	—	—	¼
Y Yellow	—	—	—	—	—	—	6	6	⅛
Z Pale orange	12	—	—	—	—	—	—	—	⅛
AA White print	—	—	—	—	3	3	—	—	⅛
Background (grays)	48	90	12	—	6	6	—	—	2
Center Aqua	—	—	—	1	—	—	—	—	scrap

Backing fabric: 4⅞ yards of 45″ wide

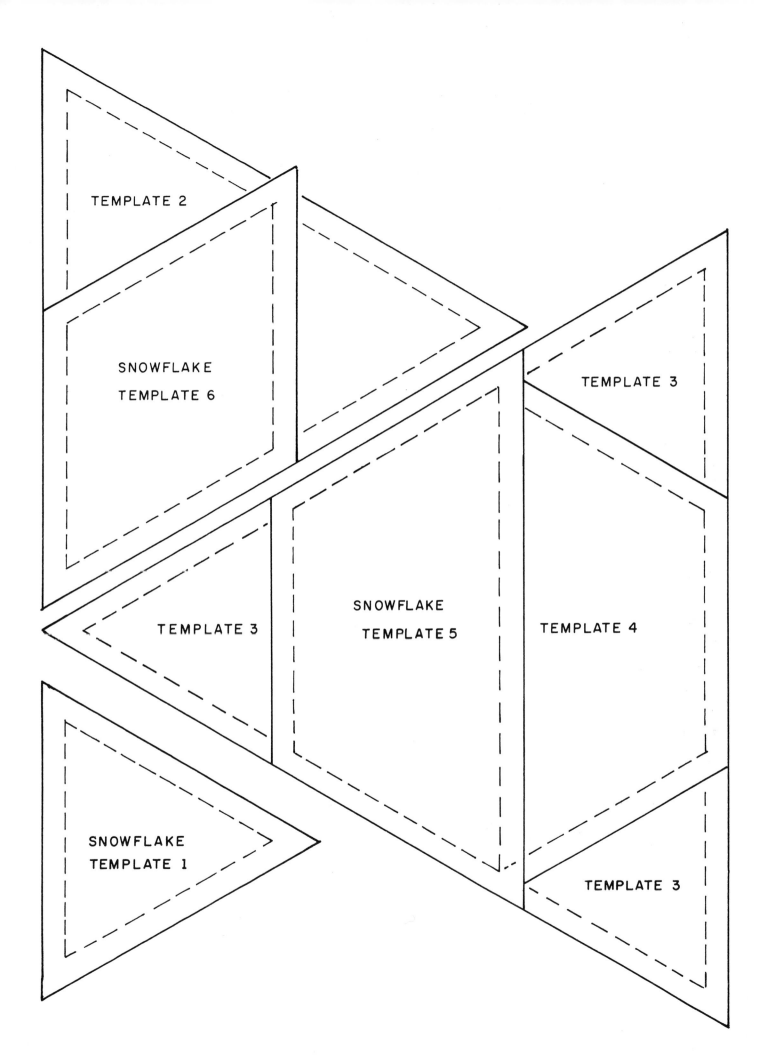

TWO TRIANGLES

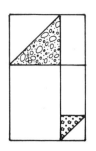

Most of the other quilts in this book are developed from traditional blocks. *Two Triangles* is produced from a very simple original design within a rectangular block format. The block is very easily constructed from two large triangles, two small triangles and three rectangles. Rectangular blocks can be set together in many straight or brickwork patterns. Try designing some blocks of your own on graph paper and playing with various arrangements.

The *Two Triangles* block is used in three different sizes in this quilt. A 22½″ by 37½″ block forms the center section. The larger triangle is green, the smaller one pink. The background is a furnishing fabric with a printed design of squares, rectangles and triangles in orange, pink, green and grays. Outline quilting along the lines of the printed design makes this large block look like many

separate pieces, while in fact there are only seven.

Surrounding the large central block are two other scales of the same pattern overlapped to produce a more complex design. The smaller blocks are 4½″ by 7½″. The medium blocks are twice that size, 9″ by 15″. In all three scales, one larger triangle is cut from green, one smaller triangle from pink.

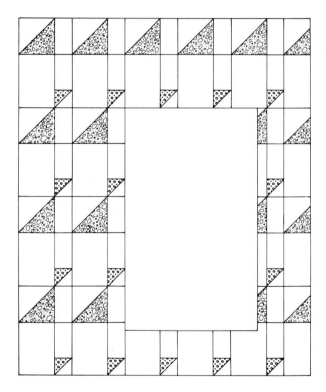

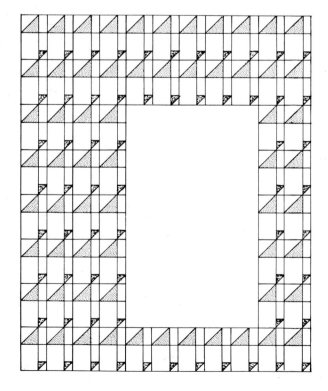

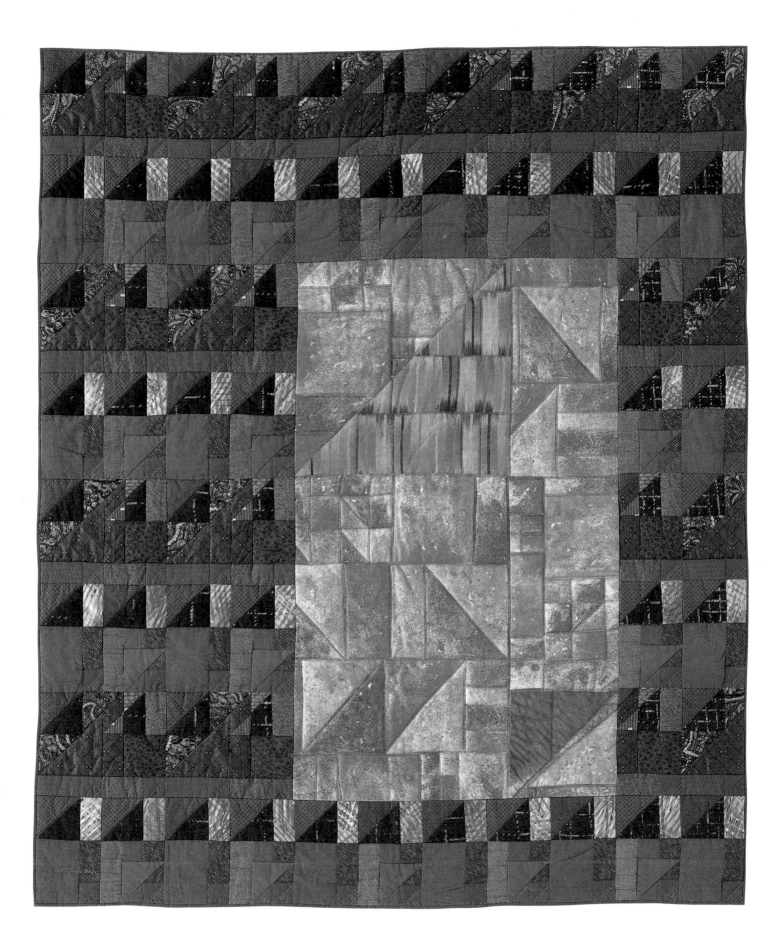

Because of the way the blocks are drawn, the pink triangles do not overlap at all. The green triangles only partially overlap. The transparency process is confined to that small overlap in the greens.

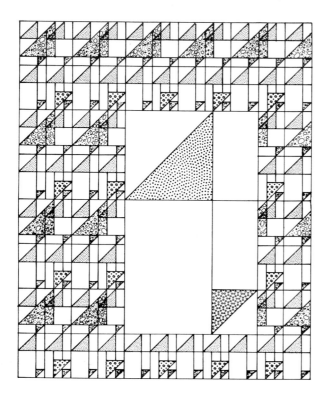

The line drawing produced by the straight overlap is quite complicated. It has been simplified above for ease of construction. Rather than using a consistent fabric for the background, I chose many medium browns with one rust, one tan print and one dull purple.

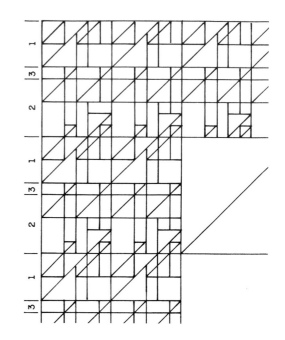

It is easier to assemble this quilt in rows rather than blocks. The rows are described in detail below with color and template maps beginning from the upper-left corner of the quilt.

Upper left corner

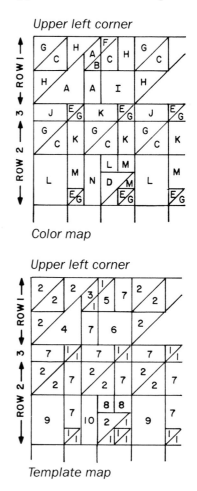

Color map

Upper left corner

Template map

Construction can be speeded up by first sewing the sub-units described here, then assembling the sub-units into the rows, and finally the rows into panels.

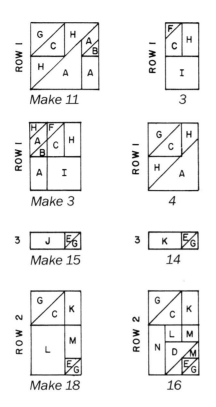

ROW 1

Make 11   3

ROW 1

Make 3   4

3   3

Make 15   14

ROW 2

ROW 2

Make 18   16

The rows are then assembled into four panels.

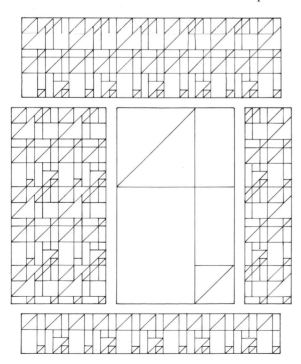

The center panel is cut from seven pieces. Because of the size of the pieces, templates are not given in this book, but here are the measurements.

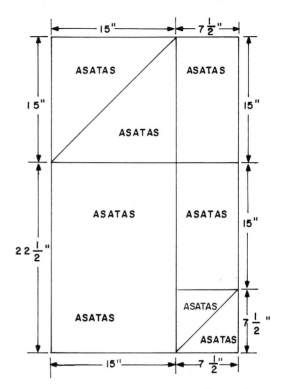

ASATAS = Add Seam Allowance To All Sides
Center panel: Make 1

This piece is sewn with quilt-as-you-go method 1 (see page 25) because the quilting lines extend right to the edges of each panel. The four outer panels are quilted with a straight machine stitch in the ditch, using an even-feed foot. The large central panel is quilted with a closed overlock machine stitch. After the quilted panels are pieced together, the back is finished by hemming fabric strips over the quilt-as-you-go seams by hand.

To make a 60½" by 50" wallhanging as illustrated here, you will need:

COLOR	TEMPLATE										YARDAGE
	1	2	3	4	5	6	7	8	9	10	
A Green	—	—	14	15	—	—	14	—	—	—	⅜
B Green	14	—	—	—	—	—	—	—	—	—	⅛
C Green	—	49	—	—	14	—	—	—	—	—	⅜
D Pink	—	16	—	—	—	—	—	—	—	—	⅛
E Pink	63	—	—	—	—	—	—	—	—	—	¼
F Rust	14	—	—	—	—	—	—	—	—	—	⅛
G Brown	63	49	—	—	—	—	—	—	—	—	½
H Brown	3	26	—	—	4	—	—	—	—	—	¼
I Purple	—	—	—	—	—	14	—	—	—	—	¼
J Brown	—	—	—	—	—	—	15	—	—	—	⅛
K Tan	—	—	—	—	—	—	48	—	—	—	½
L Brown	—	—	—	—	—	—	—	16	—	18	½
M Brown	16	—	—	—	—	—	18	16	—	—	¼
N Brown	—	—	—	—	—	—	—	—	16	—	¼

Center panel: Cut according to the measurements on page 137
Cut according to the measurements on page 137

    Background   ¾ yard

    Green triangle   ½ yard

    Pink triangle   ¼ yard

Backing fabric: 3⅛ yards of 45" wide or 1⅞ yards of 60" wide

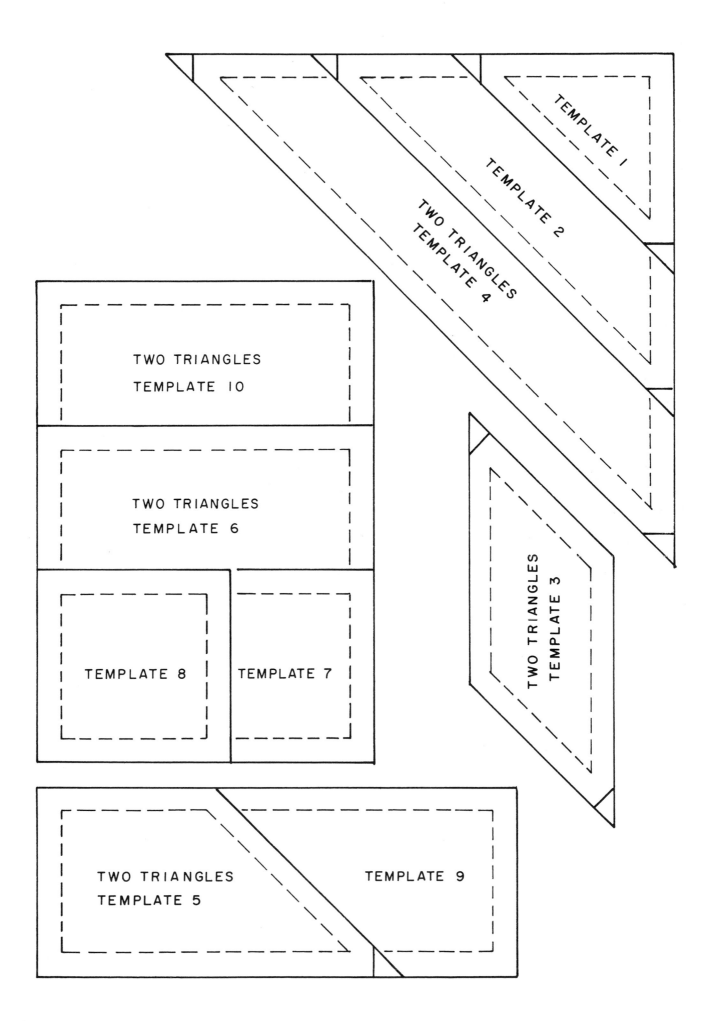

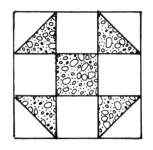

SHOO FLY

Shoo Fly is a traditional pattern based on a nine-patch. The four corner squares have been cut into triangles. *Shoo Fly* is usually set together with sashing strips and posts to form an overall design, as in this quilt.

The reverberant pattern begins with forty-nine 6″ *Shoo Fly* blocks, set together with 2″ sashing bars and peach posts.

The second pattern contains 18″ blocks with the pattern elements in yellow.

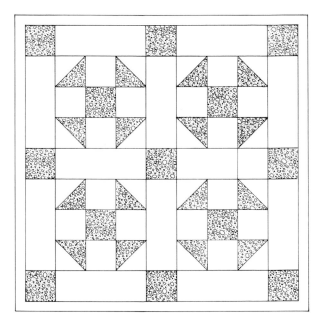

Finally, a 54″ single pattern in pink was centered on the other two.

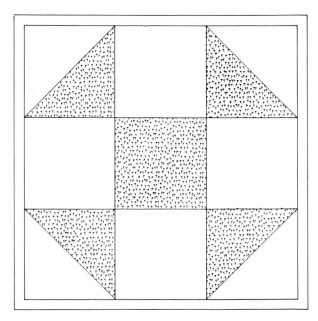

141   SHOO FLY

This is a scrap quilt made with only a modest concern for transparency. I do not find it at all necessary to make perfect transparency the overriding factor in choosing fabrics for each quilt. It is only one of several fabric selection concepts that can be operating at the same time. In *Shoo Fly*, you will find that, in general:

Color A Blue   Color AB Green
Color B Yellow   Color BC Pale orange
Color C Pink   Color ABC Grayish
Color D Peach   Color AC Lavender

This wallhanging is bordered with a band of squares (Template 2) in hot pinks, rectangles (Template 5) in a pink/green print, and an outer

4″ border of a mottled gray-green furnishing fabric.

It is interesting to put an unrelated free-hand quilted drawing on top of a pieced geometric surface (see page 27). In this quilt, a large-scale drapery print of foliage was used as the backing fabric and the quilt was machine quilted from the back along the lines of the printed design. The quilting was done free-motion using a feed-dog cover plate and darning foot. The outlines of the foliage pattern were stitched with a shaded pink cotton sewing thread. Again with free-motion on the machine, stipple quilting with gray thread added a further texture to some areas.

You may wish to make the quilt with a more careful eye toward color transparency. Here is a color map for one quarter of *Shoo Fly*:

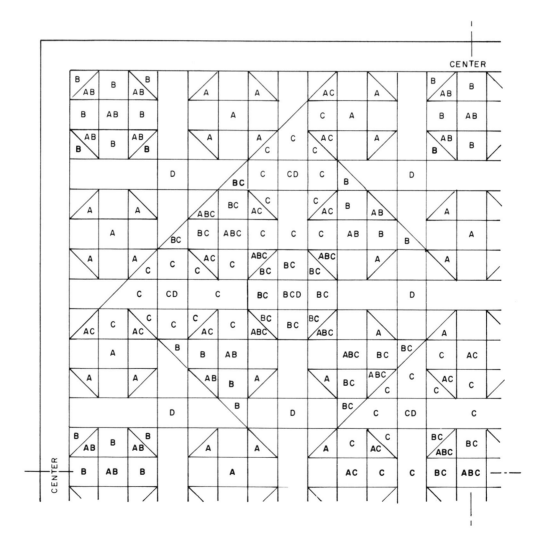

To make a 66½″ by 66½″ quilt as illustrated here, you will need:

COLOR	TEMPLATE						TOTAL YARDAGE
	1	**2**	**3**	**3R**	**4**	**5**	
A	88	20	—	—	—	—	½
B	48	48	—	—	—	—	½
C	52	52	8	8	8	4	1
D	—	4	—	—	—	—	¼
AB	40	12	—	—	—	—	¼
BC	20	28	—	—	—	—	¼
AC	40	4	—	—	—	—	¼
ABC	28	9	—	—	—	—	¼
BCD	—	4	—	—	—	—	¼
CD	—	12	—	—	—	—	¼
Background	96	100	16	16	8	24	1¾
Border	—	28	—	—	—	—	¼
	—	—	—	—	—	5	½

Outer border: 2 (58½″ by 4½″)   2

2 (66½″ by 4½″)

Backing fabric: 4 yards of 45″ wide

Back

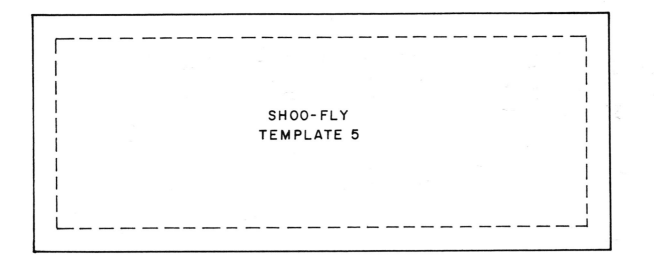

SHOO-FLY
TEMPLATE 5

SHOO-FLY
TEMPLATE 4

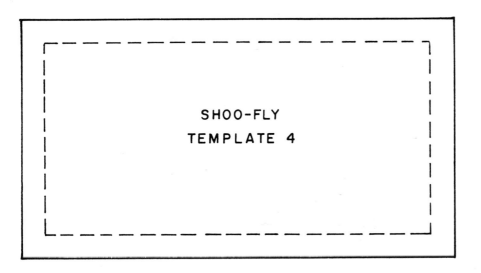

SHOO-FLY
TEMPLATE 2

SHOO-FLY
TEMPLATE 1

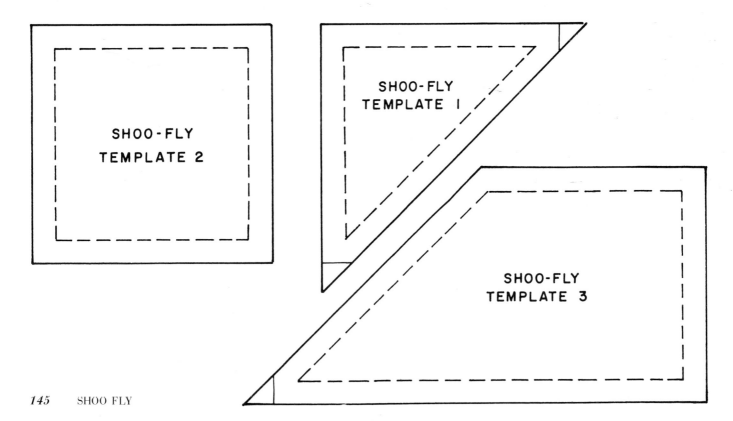

SHOO-FLY
TEMPLATE 3

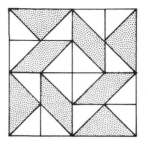

WINDBLOWN SQUARE

A traditional block with a lot of motion to it, *Windblown Square* is a pinwheel pattern easily constructed in four sections.

For this quilt, three different scales of the *Windblown Square* block were used. The first is an 8″ block arranged as a sixteen-block square.

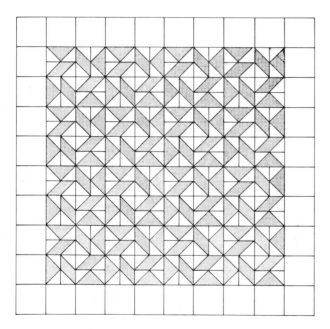

Overlaid on these are four 16″ blocks.

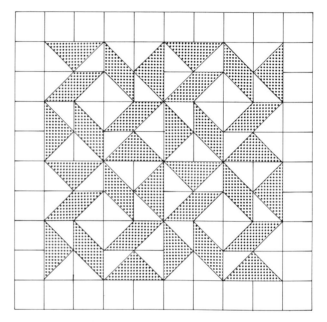

Finally, one large 32″ block is centered over the other two layers.

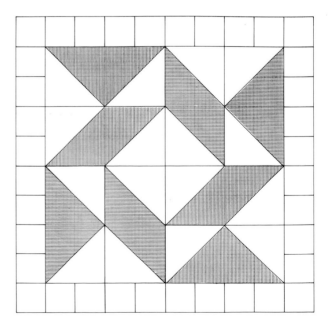

147   WINDBLOWN SQUARE

Careful examination shows that each of the four quarters of the design is the same, but rotated through 90 degrees around the center of the quilt.

In selecting the fabrics for this quilt, I did not follow a strict color transparency scheme, although there are parts of some layers visible in some sections. Many of the fabrics chosen are very busy and fine-scaled prints, different from many of the other quilts in this book.

The border blocks are an overlap of layers A and B, but without the C layer. They were drawn by continuing the first two patterns, extending them out another row. A color change in this outer row defined the border visually.

Quilting was done on the machine using two self-programmed fancy stitches.

The design in the 32″ block was outlined in a larger scale of the sawtooth stitch pattern with orange thread. A narrower sawtooth stitch outlined the 8″ block pattern, with light blue thread in the outer blocks and with chartreuse thread at the center.

Should you wish to follow a more orthodox color transparency scheme, the following chart will be helpful.

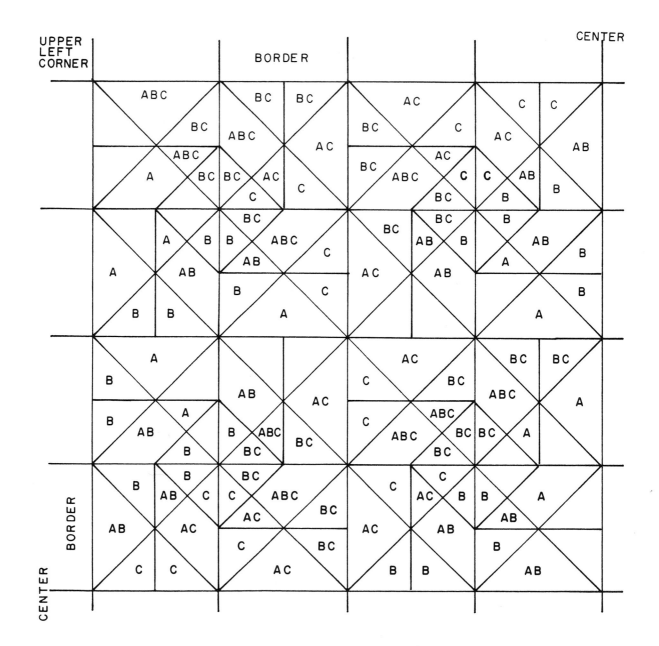

To make a 42½″ by 42½″ wallhanging, you will need:

COLOR	TEMPLATE				YARDAGE
	1	**2**	**3**	**4**	
A	16	8	—	20	¼
B	40	—	48	—	⅜
C	24	—	48	—	¼
AB	20	24	—	12	⅜
AC	16	8	—	28	⅜
BC	40	—	48	—	⅜
ABC	12	24	—	4	¼
Background	24	—	48	—	¼
Border					
A	16	20	—	16	⅜
B	36	—	20	16	⅜
AB	20	16	—	20	⅜
Background	36	—	16	20	⅜

Backing fabric: 1½ yards of 45″ wide

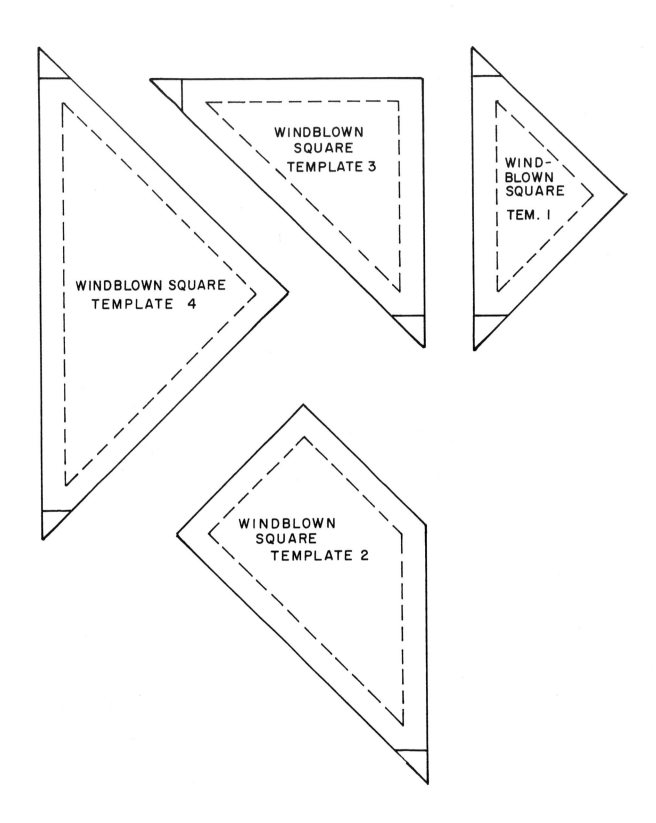

WINDBLOWN
SQUARE
TEMPLATE 3

WIND-
BLOWN
SQUARE

TEM. I

WINDBLOWN SQUARE
TEMPLATE 4

WINDBLOWN
SQUARE
TEMPLATE 2

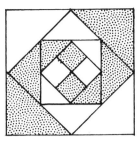

MONKEY WRENCH

The traditional *Monkey Wrench* block makes a fascinating quilt with relatively simple piecing. A pieced block of light and dark triangles and squares is set together with plain squares of light and dark fabric to form an interlocking pattern.

For this quilt, three different scales of the *Monkey Wrench* pattern are combined.

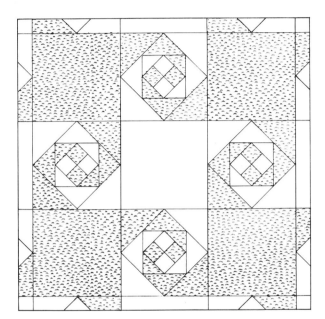

For transparency, the first pattern was made of light and dark grays, the second pattern of white and blue, and the third pattern of white and red. To keep track, set up a chart:

Light gray plus white	Light gray
Dark gray plus white	Dark gray
Light gray plus blue (plus white)	Light blue
Dark gray plus blue (plus white)	Dark blue
Light gray plus red (plus white)	Pink
Dark gray plus red (plus white)	Dark red
Light gray plus blue plus red	Lavender
Dark gray plus blue plus red	Purple

Make yourself a map of the final design with each piece marked with its correct color.

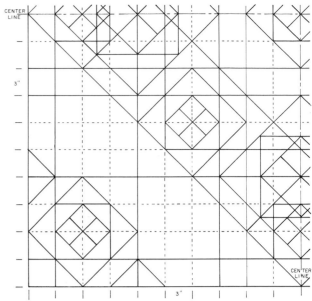

A quilt of this complexity requires careful construction. There are a very large number of templates involved. The best way to construct such a quilt is to draw a large portion of the design at full size on graph paper. In this case, the four quadrants of the design are the same pattern of lines, but colored differently. Drawing one quarter of the quilt at full size on graph paper will suffice to give you all of the templates. The drawing below is based on a 3″ grid which will produce a 60″ square pieced center. With a 6″ border on each size, the quilt will finish 72″ by 72″.

Because of the multilayered complexity of the design, there is a lot to look at in this quilt. The light/dark pattern is readily apparent. The large arms of red/pink are also easily distinguished. The blue pattern is more subtle and requires some searching. The three separate scales of reverberant pattern resonate with the complexity of the piece.

The quilting on this *Monkey Wrench* is done by hand with red, blue and gray thread outlining and filling in the layers of pattern. An 80% cotton-20% polyester batting was used, resulting in a very flat surface. For ease in hand quilting, make sure to rinse and dry this batting before use, according to the instructions in the package.

Picking out a quilting design for a particular piece is another place where careful thought will reward you. In this case, the quilt was already so complicated, a quilting pattern was chosen to outline each of the scales of pattern.

This quilt is recommended only for the very experienced quilter who is ready to begin the process of drafting a full-size pattern and constructing templates. Yardages will vary, depending on the number of fabrics used.

DOUBLE T

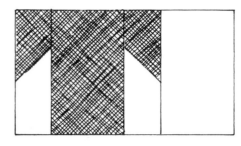

The *Double T* forms an overall design rather than discrete blocks. It is usually made of light and dark fabrics.

For this quilt (made as a wallhanging), three different scales of the pattern were chosen, but none were mathematical multiples of another.

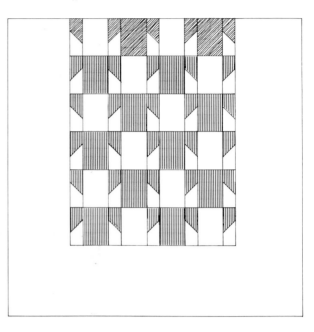

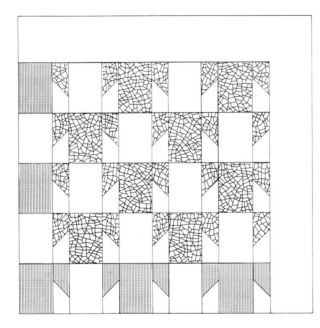

A full-size drawing of the quilt was made on gridded vellum (see page 19).

The starting place for fabric selection was the brown fabric with black lines and dots. This is a heavy cotton canvas furnishing fabric from the 50's or 60's and had been on the shelf for quite a while. It came originally from a church rummage sale, along with a couple of curtains that someone had made from it. The pattern pieces for the quilt were cut randomly from the brown fabric. In fact, they were cut from the back of the fabric, where none of the black showed. In arranging the brown pieces on the design wall, I placed the more densely figured ones at the bottom.

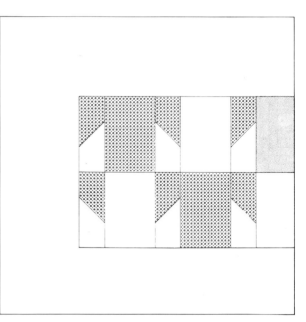

155   DOUBLE T

The blue fabric with black lines, arcs, gold bits and red triangles comes from the same era as the brown and black canvas. It was a five-yard remnant at $1 per yard of a very fine cotton furnishing fabric, 36″ wide. The fabric was originally on a grayish-green background and has been shared with some friends who have used it in all kinds of different ways. A few years ago, a small piece was experimentally overdyed with blue fiber-reactive dye; this quilt used every scrap of that piece.

The three *Double T* scales of pattern have been extended into the border on this quilt, but in a much subtler value range.

I loved the whimsical patterns on the brown and blue cottons and wanted to unite and emphasize them with the quilting. This was done by free-motion quilting on the machine in black thread with a darning foot and feed-dog cover plate. The machine quilting forms doodles on the surface of the quilt, outlining the printed shapes, extending them and drawing more. Most of this was done free-hand. The thin black lines have been stitched over twice to thicken them.

The borders were then free-motion quilted in a tiny erratic zig zag pattern, giving the effect of stipple quilting. The threads used for stippling were 50 weight cotton in cream, light blue, light pink and light gray. A ¼″ black binding defined the edge.

The machine quilting of this *Double T* added a lot of detail to the pieced top. When all of the quilting was done, the center of the piece seemed to lack a definite focus. To adjust this, I added a little white textile paint to one of the central blue rectangles.

This *Double T* quilt is recommended only for the very experienced quilter. You will have to make a full-size drawing of the entire quilt, with your selected overlaps, as the piece work is different in every part. (See page 19 for a description of graph-paper construction.) Very careful labeling of each piece of the quilt will also be needed to keep the color transparencies straight. With none

of the piece work or colors repeating in an orderly way, this quilt requires extraordinary thought and patience to assemble. *Double T*, as I have drawn it, is based on three scales of pattern. The rectangle that forms the center of the T is 6″ by 9″ in the red layer, 8″ by 12″ in the brown layer and 12″ by 18″ in the blue layer.

Although this *Double T* quilt combines three unrelated scales of reverberant pattern, all three are aligned vertically. Diagrammed below is a sketch for a different quilt drawn from the same three patterns, but this time varying the angles. I find this drawing fascinating, but it would be enormously difficult to construct as a pieced quilt.

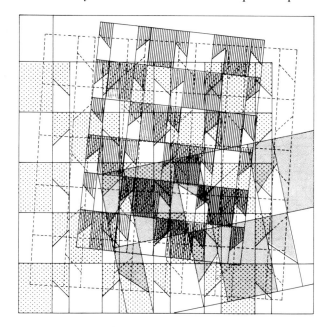

The liveliness of the designs produced by angling the grids of pattern in this way is very exciting. Careful selection of blocks and angles may lead to some quilt designs using odd angles that are easier to sew; or perhaps this is a place where appliqué or paint can take over.

An additional layer of pattern is applied to this sketched *Double T* by repeating the brown scale of pattern in quilting stitches at yet another angle. How to draw such a quilting design is described on page 28.

Back

CONCLUSION

I hope that you have found this process for expanding the range of quilt pattern design as exciting as I have in preparing this book. Most of these quilts are developed from very simple traditional blocks. There are many other possibilities for fascinating quilts within these same blocks. For instance, try using the idea of a layer of mirrored blocks, as I did with *Clay's Choice*, with the *King's Crown* or *Two Triangles* blocks. Experiment with a diagonal grid like the one in *Roman Square* in a layer of *Jacob's Ladder, Corn and Beans* or *Prairie Queen*. The *Snowflake* pattern might be very interesting if the larger snowflake layer were rotated 30 degrees. *Roman Square* and *Shoo Fly* can be formed with uneven scales of pattern in the way that *Monkey Wrench* and *Double T* have been.

There are hundreds of other traditional quilt blocks to try. A simple *Log Cabin* block could be set with a diagonal layer as in *Roman Square*. Try a *Variable Star* in overlapped layers similar to this *Shoo Fly*; or *Dutchman's Puzzle* set like *Clay's Choice*. For a real exercise in mastering color transparency, see if you can make a *Baby's Blocks* quilt with a second layer as I did in *Mill Wheel I* while keeping the colors and values in the proper places.

Snowflake and *Two Triangles* are original blocks. One uses a hexagon and one a rectangle for its block shape. A square would work equally well as a block and is a familiar shape with which to begin designing your own blocks. Combine your blocks into quilts using some of the ideas developed here.

Reverberant pattern design can clearly be applied to all kinds of designs not involving repeated blocks, and to many other areas of surface design as well. Various layers of pattern can be adapted, warped, mirrored or decomposed in many different ways. As a source of exciting and innovative designs, the field is open and the territory almost completely unexplored.

PATTERN on PATTERN

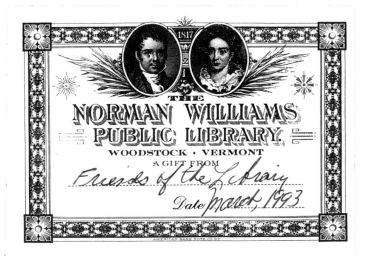

RUTH B. MCDOWELL

PATTERN

Simply the Best

*W*hen we started our publishing efforts in 1983, we made one pledge to ourselves: to produce the finest quilt books imaginable. The critics and our loyal readers clearly believe that we're living up to that promise.

In a time when thin, 64-page quilt books with only staples to hold their pages intact and small numbers of color photos sell for as much as $19.95, we are proud that our books set a noticeably higher standard.

Books from The Quilt Digest Press are hefty, with many more pages and masses of color photos. They are printed on high-quality satin-finish paper and are bound with durable glues and spines to last a lifetime. The world's finest quilt photographer does all our work. A great design team lavishes its attention on every detail of every page. And the world's finest commercial printer sees to it that every book is a gem. Add knowledgeable authors with vital ideas and you, too, will say, "The Quilt Digest Press? Oh, they're Simply the Best."

Try another of our books. They're as good as the one in your hands. And write for our free color catalogue.

THE QUILT DIGEST PRESS

Dept. D
P.O. Box 1331
Gualala, CA 95445